HOW TO PASS THE EMIRATES CABIN CREW INTERVIEW

An Inside Look at the Emirates Interview
Process, and what it Takes to Succeed

R. J. HOGAN

ISBN-13: 978-1494875657 ISBN-10: 1494875659

Published by V1 Consulting

Anchorage, AK

All rights reserved. No part of this book may be reproduced or transmitted in any form or by any means, electronic or mechanical, including photocopying, recording, or by any information storage and retrieval system, without written permission from the author, except for the inclusion of brief quotations in a review.

Unattributed quotations attributed to R. J. Hogan

©Copyright 2014

First Edition

Library of Congress Cataloguing-in Publication Data has been applied for

INTRODUCTION	**1**
PART I: INTERVIEW BASICS	**8**
THE BIG PICTURE: WHAT IS EXPECTED FROM CABIN CREWMEMBERS?	8
THE ONLINE APPLICATION	13
MAKING FIRST IMPRESSIONS	20
DRESS FOR SUCCESS	23
GROOMING	33
PHYSIQUE	41
SELLING YOURSELF: ACTIONS SPEAK (MUCH!) LOUDER THAN WORDS	44
PHYSICAL REQUIREMENTS	71
PART II: THE EMIRATES INTERVIEW	**73**
VIDEO AND QA	77
THE RESUME HANDOVER	81
FIRST GROUP DYNAMIC	85
YEAS OR NAYS	95
ENGLISH COMPREHENSION AND APTITUDE TESTS	97
ADVANCED GROUP DYNAMIC	106
ONE ON ONE INTERVIEW	114
CLOSING THE INTERVIEW	121
PHYSICALS	124
CONCLUSION	**126**

Introduction

Congratulations! By starting this book, you are taking the first step toward an exciting, life-changing (for the better!) career, one of the most unique you'll ever experience. This book and the path you are about to take will help lead you to Emirates as an international flight attendant. In the airline industry, we refer to the "new you" as cabin crew. Like all paths that take you somewhere new, it can be long, and will at times require effort on your part. This book will be your companion on this journey, and like any good travel partner, it will help you arrive at your goal.

Getting this job is important to you; the fact that you are reading this book is a testament to that. And it should be. A cabin crew job at Emirates is truly a great and unique opportunity.

Because this is such a tremendous opportunity, you might be asking yourself, "Can I trust what's written here? Why should I believe anything this book has to say?"

I have been involved in airline industry interviews for quite a while. I have interviewed (successfully) and *been* interviewed many times, more than enough to have intimate knowledge of how to pass an interview. Beyond my personal experiences, the information you will read shortly is *ALL* based on the actual individual experiences of applicants who have successfully completed the *exact* process you are attempting.

There is one other reason I wrote this book (and several others like it): my utter frustration at watching quality candidates lose their chance at their dream job because of the most basic mistakes. The job of human resources (HR) is to hire, not to bid farewell to qualified applicants. But if someone commits a gaffe in an interview, HR has no other alternative but to not hire. I cannot tell you the number of times I have personally sat there and screamed internally at applicants that just disqualified themselves for simple mistakes, "Why, oh why, did you just do that?"

Reading this book and sticking to the rules outlined herein will put you ahead of the competition. Way ahead. This book is not meant to be shiny, glossy, or full of meaningless fluff. This book covers all the subjects that are critical components for your preparation and ultimate success.

All that being said, let us begin:

Would you like a career that flies you to major cities all over the world, setting up reservations for you in four and five star hotels? When you check in to your hotel, do you want someone to hand you an envelope full of local currency for dinner, drinks, gifts, etc.?

What if that same career paid for your living accommodations, utilities, and then shuttled you to and from work, all while you're living right in the middle of one of the world's most iconic cities--famous beaches, nightclubs, shopping, restaurants, and more? Free medical coverage, thirty days of paid vacation, travel benefits around the world, retirement fund, end of service bonus, and the list goes on.

Does all that sounds too good to be true? It may, but believe it or not, it's also totally attainable. Traveling all over the world and staying in world-class hotels (and getting paid to do it!) is like an example from "Lifestyles of the Rich and Famous." Living a life like this is unimaginable unless you're a movie star or the next hot pop-music sensation, right?

So how do you get it? Everything I have just described is part of the benefits package for all entry-level cabin crew at the United Arab EMIRATES' premier airline. And Emirates is hiring a lot of cabin crew members, which is great for you.

I'm not exaggerating; being a cabin crewmember with Emirates, and the opportunities it provides, are absolutely fantastic. Here's a very important point to remember about fantastic jobs: *everyone wants one.*

Emirates knows that. These cabin crew jobs are very competitive, very hard to get, and there is no shortage of applicants. A cabin crew position at Emirates is a once in a lifetime opportunity, and can be either a lifelong career or purely a three-year free world tour, depending on your long-term goals. The majority of applicants that turn out for recruiting events (Open Days) for cabin crew interviews are not successful. Typically, only around 5% (and in some case only 2-3%!) of attendees are hired. That means that if 1000 applicants turn out for an Open Day, *at most* around fifty will head to Dubai for employment.

After reading that number, some of you may be put off.

"Only *fifty* get hired? Those aren't good odds," you may be thinking.

That is where this book comes in handy.

Why are so many applicants unsuccessful? For one simple reason: *they show up to the Open Day totally unprepared.*

Think about the very brief list of benefits I mentioned above (which is only a fraction of the total package). This is truly a unique and enviable career with one of the top companies in the world. Emirates interviews candidates from countries all around the world, and they can be as picky as they want. Can you walk into a competitive interview setting like this without preparing, and be successful? Such a scenario is very, very unlikely.

Which is great!

"Why is that great?" you may ask.

If the majority of applicants are unprepared, and you are thoroughly prepared, it's easy to stand out for all the right reasons. And your preparation begins now.

Competing for a job like this, and being successful, requires you to be completely prepared for the screening process. You need to present yourself in the best possible way, and you don't have a lot of time or chances to do it. In the very short period of time you have available, you must demonstrate the qualities HR wants to see in its cabin crew.

You will now have an advantage over the other 999 applicants showing up at your recruiting event. You will understand how to give the best possible performance and show your interviewers what they want to see. This book describes in detail what you need to do

We will cover what to bring, your personal presentation, what interviewers are looking for, and how to show it to them.

This is the most important concept to keep in mind: *this book is not a cheat*! The title is not "How to fool your interviewers and trick them into hiring you." There is no way to "beat" the process, there is only a way to prepare for the process. With the inside knowledge this book covers, you will be better prepared than any of your peers. Preparation for the interview takes time and effort, but it is time and effort well spent. Put the work in now. The results will be worth the sacrifice.

This book covers many aspects of good interview techniques. You will learn the importance of making a good first impression and how to do it. We will cover specific stages of the cabin crew interview, to include:

- ✓ Depending on the location of the open day event you are attending, it may require an invitation through the online application. You will understand how to fill out online forms correctly and the importance of doing so.
- ✓ What human resource representatives are looking for during the "Question time" following the company promotion video
- ✓ How to handle the all-important "resume handover," a twenty second opportunity for HR to start the YES or NO process.

How to Pass the Emirates Cabin Crew Interview

- ✓ How to behave during group dynamic exercises when applicants are divided into smaller groups and observed during their discussions.
- ✓ How to prepare for the English comprehension test.
- ✓ How to prepare for the aptitude test.
- ✓ Finally, we will discuss how to effectively present yourself and formulate great answers to the airline-specific interview questions.

Part I: Interview Basics

The big picture: what is expected from cabin crewmembers?

Before we get into the meat of the "Inside Scoop," it's important to cover the basics. These basic interview concepts will get you over the first hurdle and to the second day, which is covered in detail later. Some of these concepts may be obvious, but their importance should never be underestimated. A thorough review is essential.

Before we start on how to apply, you need to understand the role you're trying to fill. What exactly are cabin crew supposed to do? Serve drinks? Fluff pillows? As you probably guessed, there's a lot more to it than that. We will begin there.

You're trying to become cabin crew for one of the world's most prestigious airlines. The first step is having a clear understanding of what that job requires and what will be expected of you. After all, you can't show HR what they want to see if you don't understand what they're looking for.

How to Pass the Emirates Cabin Crew Interview

Emirates has built its reputation on uncompromising luxury, service, and presentation to its customers. The company relies on you to provide the extremely high level of service its customers are accustomed to. A cabin crew position includes great benefits, there's no doubt, but with those benefits come strict standards and high expectations for its employees. What does the company expect from you, as cabin crew, in particular?

You are THE face of front line customer service, and from that standpoint you are the most important part of the airline. When passengers think back on their travel experience, especially when they're deciding which company to book their insanely expensive first class ticket to Paris with, who will they think about? It won't be the pilots. They sit in their tiny room in the front of the aircraft pushing buttons and making the occasional PA announcement. Who really knows what they're doing up there? It also won't be the gate or ticket agents. Passengers have a very brief exchange with them, checking in and boarding, and that's it. The face your passengers associate with their travel experience will be yours and your fellow cabin crew. When passengers book and re-book tickets, it will be based mainly on your interaction with them. Emirates relies on you, personally, to insure their revenue stream. Studies show the single biggest negative memory passengers retain from a flight is an unfriendly experience with cabin crew. People forget about long delays, bad food, and cramped seats, but never bad service.

You will be expected to provide outstanding customer service on long flights all around the world, regardless of the time of day or how you personally feel at any given moment. Simultaneously, you are responsible for providing for the safety of each and every passenger on board your flight. That may not sound challenging right now, but it can be. There will be long nights when you can barely keep your eyes open, but you still have to go get champagne for the passenger is 33C with a smile on your face. You will have to happily deal with unpleasant passengers who've drunk too much, are just flat-out rude, or don't use enough (if any) toothpaste. You will have to be ready for any emergency situation, all while maintaining your composure and professionalism.

A drunken man just threw up on a screaming baby. You'll have to deal with that, as well as clean up the mess. Situations like this are unpleasant, but they can and will happen. You'll have to smile while you mop up the vomit.

The flight crew (pilots) call back to inform you the aircraft is on fire and you're landing in the ocean. While this may alarm you personally, the passengers are looking at you and judging your composure. If you panic, they panic. If you can't control your outward composure, on top of the emergency water landing, you will have mass hysteria. As cabin crew, you must keep your composure at all times, no matter what. Particularly in emergencies, people will look to you for guidance, and you must provide it.

These are some of the qualities your assessors and interviewers are looking for. You must convince them that you are capable of all this and more.

Think about the billboards, TV commercials, and magazine ads that you see advertising for Emirates. There is almost always a smiling, vibrant member of the cabin crew featured prominently in these ads. This is the image the company promotes around the world. As you prepare for your Open Day, picture yourself in one of these ads. This is the fundamental image you need to present to your interviewers. They need to be able to picture you in the company's uniform on a billboard in Paris or New York, as a visual representation of the high level of service Emirates provides.

The qualities cabin crew are specifically expected to exhibit are: professional, empathetic, progressive, visionary, and cosmopolitan. Everything you say and do during your assessments must reinforce the embodiment of these qualities.

Points to remember

- ✓ Cabin crew members have two primary functions: provide exceptional customer service, no matter what, and ensure the safety of every passenger on board the aircraft.
- ✓ Picture the image of cabin crew members you see in advertisements for Emirates; this is the image you must portray to the assessment team.

The online application

First things first: you really want this job if you're taking the time to read this book, so I'm assuming you've filled out the online application. I'm going to say this, however, because there are always people who show up to Open Days off the cuff and haven't done any preparation beforehand. If you have filled out the application in advance, and done it correctly, it makes a much better case for your interest level for this job.

You may think filling out an online application is a no-brainer, but you are wrong. The *majority* of applicants that fill out online applications make some kind of error; whether it's a misspelling, typographical error, missed data field, or incorrect data. Take some time filling out the application. Don't try and do it all on your fifteen minute lunch break at your current job.

Once you complete the online application, have someone *else* proofread it. It's almost impossible to proofread your own work. Anytime you write anything, whether it's a book or just a paragraph on why you want to work for Emirates, *you* know exactly what you're trying to say. If you are proofreading your own work, your brain will automatically fill in missing or misspelled words to complete your thoughts. You really must have someone else proofread what you've written or you'll miss mistakes. Another tip is to look at what you have written by reading it backwards – your brain will catch any words that are missing or out of place.

One section of the online application asks for a letter of application where you give the reasons you want to work for Emirates. To that end, honesty is the best policy. To a point! You don't necessarily need to fill them in on the fact that the bank is sending you nasty letters (it's okay, we've all been there once or twice) or that your abusive ex-partner is stalking you. Stick to safe subjects and nothing too extreme; focus on the points that have inspired you to seek this exciting life of new people and destinations. Remember this going forward from this point: avoid personal drama in any way during the interview/application process. The less drama you convey to Emirates, the safer you are for them to invest in.

The remaining sections of the application ask for contact information, education history, and work history. Most of the paperwork correspondence is done through email, but occasionally by phone call. Make sure you fill out every applicable field, and the information is correct.

Some Open Day events, depending on the country, will allow walk-in applicants. Can you walk in off the street and be successful in the process? Yes, you can. All things being equal, who do you think will have the better chance at getting hired? The person that simply strolls in off the street or the one that has taken the time to apply online, brings a professional resume, works on their personal performance and presentation, etc? You can walk in and maybe things will work out. You are much more likely to be successful, however, if you take the time to prepare beforehand and apply online.

Dress up your contact information

You're ready to start the process, or maybe you already have. Take a moment and consider your contact information. The company can and will be communicating with you via phone, voicemail, email, and possibly snail mail. Make sure the contact information you provide is accurate, and that you can, in fact, be contacted using them.

Case in point: a young gentleman I know had a great opportunity at a world-class company. He submitted an online application, but provided a contact number that he didn't check very often. A few weeks later, when he did get around to checking the voicemail for that number, there were a series of messages from the company trying to call him in for an interview. By the time he returned the call, there were no more interview slots available, and they were clearly annoyed by the tardiness of his response. It was an expensive lesson for him. Make sure you provide a good number and a good address that you're actively using.

One word on email addresses: just because your address has been cutebuns99@mail.com for the last several years does *not* mean it's a good choice for a job application. I know it's inconvenient to have to check yet another email address, but come up with something professional you can include in your application packet.

The most important contact Emirates will initiate with you is known as the "Golden Call," that life-changing moment when a member of the HR team gets to deliver the good news. You can't get the "Golden Call" if your contact information isn't current. Ensure that it is, and when it changes, then update it.

CV (Resume)

You will be asked to provide a *curriculum vitae* during Open Day, also referred to as a CV or resume. That's not a big deal, unless you've never had to provide a resume in a professional setting before. Here's what you need to know about good resumes:

A resume is not a cover letter, nor a rambling narrative describing why you want to be employed by Emirates, have a flat in Dubai, and generally live like a rock star. It should *not* be multiple pages stapled together. It should *not* be written on anything except white paper.

Reviewers spend no more than an average of six seconds scanning your resume. They don't want to spend any more time than that, and if they have to, it will annoy them. Knowing that, your resume must show them everything they need to see in that six second window.

An effective resume should be a clear, concise document that summarizes your skills and qualifications. A reviewer should be able to easily scan your resume and find all the information they need clearly presented without having to dig too deep. A resume should only be one page. Reviewers don't want to flip through a packet. The resume should only contain bullet-point items pertinent to the position for which you are applying. The following is a good example of a clear, concise cabin crew resume:

Paula Scholes
265 Rhode Avenue
Miami, FL 27367
Telephone: (321) 256-2572
Email ID: paula_sc@yahoo.com

Objective:

Serving passengers as Flight Attendant properly and expanding my experiences for further career in reputed airlines.

Skills and Qualifications:

- Experienced in working as a flight attendant
- Experienced in serving passengers
- Able to demonstrate safety procedures properly
- Excellent knowledge of safety flight procedures
- Good communication skills
- Capable of working in long time

Educational Background:

- Bachelor Degree of Communication Science, University of Missouri, 2003
- Flight Attendant Course and Training, SMART Training Center, 2004

Working Experience

Flight Attendant, RTO Airlines, New Jersey, 2009-present
Responsibilities-

- Give good services for passengers
- Greet passengers and confirm tickets
- Serve food and beverages to passengers
- Demonstrate safety and emergencies such as using seatbelts, life jacket, etc.
- Announce information to passengers
- Help passengers with their goods and luggage
- Answer passenger's questions about the flight, travel routes, schedules, etc.
- Check for ensuring personal equipment of passengers such as blanket, reading material, emergency equipment and other supplies
- Give special service for children, elderly and disabled persons

How to Pass the Emirates Cabin Crew Interview

As with everything in this process, pay attention to detail when formulating your resume. Make sure the spelling and syntax are all correct. Don't try to add too much fluff, just a general synopsis of education and work experience. Include any relevant training or experience specific to being a cabin crew member, if you have any.

Resumes are usually printed on paper stock between 20lb and 24lb. What does that mean? The plain white paper they stock in the copying machine at the local Kinko's looks cheap, feels cheap, is cheap. It tears and creases easily. Use a heavier weight paper for resumes because it has more of a quality feel to it. Generally, the higher the compensation of the job you're applying for, the better the paper. Don't use anything over 24lb. Paper that thick and heavy is considered card stock and not appropriate for a resume. Don't use anything that's not white or slightly off white. Colors, designs, packets, glitter, pictures, and anything else you think of that *isn't* a one-page resume on white paper is not acceptable.

Points to remember

✓ Create a clear, concise resume. It should be no more than one page in length, on a quality white paper.

Making first impressions

Studies show that first impressions of an individual are formed in less than four seconds. You can't really ask or answer many questions in four seconds, so what does that tell you about first impressions? They are formed almost entirely from visual, non-verbal cues. How you look, the way you're dressed, the way you walk, how you smell (easy on the fragrance), and how you greet someone after an introduction are all major contributors to forming a positive first impression.

Studies also show that once that first impression has been formed, it is almost impossible to reverse. Meaning: if you start out on the wrong foot, your interview is basically done. If they don't like what they see in the first four seconds, nothing you say or do after that will change their minds. It's just human nature.

I'm asked with some frequency what is the most important aspect of interviewing effectively. The answer is making a solid first impression. I cannot overstate how critical this is. I've personally interviewed many people that make bad first impressions, whether it's a weak handshake, chewing gum in the interview, or sloppy paperwork (just to name a few). It absolutely does not matter how well the interview goes after that.

Once that opinion has formed in the mind of your interviewer, which happens in a matter of seconds, the result is basically carved in stone.

There isn't one singular component to making a good first impression; it's a combination of everything you present. How you are dressed, how you speak, how you greet, if you've filled out online forms correctly. Everything, *every single aspect of how you look and act,* contribute to the all-important first impression.

Think about this from the interviewer's perspective: they must screen *literally* hundreds of applicants in a day. If someone slouches up to their table and gives a weak hello and limp handshake, they don't have the time to dig any deeper. They can't find out that deep down inside this person is really a unique snowflake. They just don't have the time to invest. One quick initial look, and if someone doesn't fit the mold, it's on to the next one.

The sections that follow provide guidance on not just the first impression, but ensuring the overall impression you leave is a great one. Each aspect is important. Don't skip over the paperwork section because you're more interested in what to wear. Remember, it's the total package they are looking at. There are no parts that are less important than the others.

Points to remember

- ✓ Making a positive first impression is one of the most important aspects of interviewing successfully.
- ✓ There is no one point that is more or less important than the others. You will be evaluated on everything taken together as a whole.

Dress for success

You are trying to secure a highly competitive, professional, career-level position at a company that is extremely conscious of cabin crew appearance. Every aspect of what cabin crew wear while on duty is strictly controlled: from how to apply makeup to what jewelry can and can't be visible. Fully half of this job is about visual presentation. You absolutely must look the part. You can't wear the party dress you use for going out to clubs. You can't wear the suit from your secondary school graduation that doesn't quite fit. You must wear professional business attire. It should be something similar in style to the cabin crew uniforms the company uses, and conservative in nature. You need the assessment team to be able to picture you dressed in their uniform.

The point of your interview attire is not to be trendy, flashy, or otherwise remarkable. It shouldn't glow in the dark. There shouldn't be neon logos all over it. Emirates are very strict on cabin crew uniform requirements; every crew member must look the same. This is not the time to express your individuality and uniqueness through your dress.

Women's dress standards

The standard cabin crew uniform for ladies is a suit and skirt ensemble. This is what you should wear for Open and Assessment Days. The crew uniform is a light tan. Showing up in a suit that is nearly identical in color to the cabin crew uniform is a little corny. A suit and skirt ensemble in black, grey, or navy blue is a good conservative choice. You can't go wrong with those colors. You can go wrong with something else. That red pantsuit your mom wore back in the 90s is not a good choice (but it's free!). You need your assessors to picture you in the cabin crew uniform, and the easiest way to do that is with a conservative colored suit.

Your blouse should be white or cream in color, nothing flamboyant or flashy. It should not reflect light, sparkle, or show what's underneath. It should be made of cotton or a cotton-blend. The shirt should completely cover your bra, and should be buttoned one button above the cleavage line.

You may be thinking, "I'm only going to wear this suit one time for my assessment, so I don't want to spend a lot of money on it."

How to Pass the Emirates Cabin Crew Interview

This should not be the cheapest set of clothes you've ever purchased.

You need to look at this suit like an investment. Spending some time and money getting a nice suit is the first step in getting a job thousands and thousands of people would love to have. Don't go cheap.

The ensemble should be made from wool or a wool blend. Do not buy a polyester suit. It will wrinkly easily, and over the course of the day will look cheap and worn; a cheap, worn applicant is not the impression you want to give.

The suit absolutely must be tailored. You can buy something off a rack, which will be less expensive, but make sure you have it tailored. Remember, your assessors literally see thousands of applicants trying to become cabin crew members. Cabin crew uniforms are carefully fitted, and they are trying to picture you wearing the uniform in their head. It will be immediately obvious to them if your suit is fitted or not.

You're not going to be wearing this suit to nightclubs or out on dates. You're going to be wearing this suit to interview for a very conservative, image conscious company. The skirt should fall to the middle of the knee, no longer and definitely no shorter. The shorter the skirt, the faster the exit--remember that.

Shoes should be conservative in color and have a medium heel. By conservative in color, think black or brown. Not red, not sequined, and not with bling all over them.

How high a heel should your shoes have? Think of heel-height like Goldilock's bed: they shouldn't be too high or too low. They should be just right, which is somewhere between the two. Flat shoes look like sandals. Stiletto heels look slutty. Just to put it into perspective, female cabin crew members change into their red leather company-issued flat shoes during the flight and then back into the medium heels for boarding and disembarking. This should give some insight into how Emirates wants female crewmembers to look to the public eye.

Similar to the skirt, think "the higher the heel, the quicker the exit." Wear a medium heel, black or brown. I know I mentioned this before, but it happens a lot, so I'll say it again: DO NOT wear red stiletto heels, no matter how good you think they look. DO NOT wear white shoes, and DO NOT wear calf-high leather boots. Think about the images of cabin crew ladies on the billboard. Are they wearing shoes with sparkly jewels all over them? I assure you that they are not.

You should wear stockings and they should be nude. This matches the cabin crew uniform. White stocking ARE NOT nude. Neither are black stockings. Nude stockings match your skin tone, so make sure to buy an appropriate set.

Men's dress standards

Since you probably skipped over the section for women, I'll reiterate a few points. The EK male cabin crew uniform is a dark brown suit, but you don't want to try to copy the uniform identically, as this comes off a bit cheesy. Black, navy blue, or charcoal-grey are all good interview suit colors. Quality and fit of a suit are very important, especially for men. Pick something made from wool or a wool blend. I know polyester is considerably cheaper, and while you're comparing it to a wool suit on the rack they may look the same, but they are not. At the end of a long assessment day, a polyester suit will look like a wrinkly mess that you may or may not have slept in last night. Think of your suit as an investment that will pay dividends for years down the road. Spend some money up front on a good one.

Make sure you have your suit tailored. Suits are produced to generic dimensions, initially, and if you don't have it fit specifically for you, it will be apparent. Don't wear your brother's suit, or try to pick the best one you can find at the local thrift shop.

The shirt and tie that go under the suit are equally important parts of your attire. Your shirt should be white or possibly light blue. You can't go wrong with those colors. You can go wrong with something else.

"But wait! I have a really nice purple shirt and tie that look great with my suit. Can't I wear that?"

Read the previous paragraph. You can't go wrong with a white or (LIGHT!) blue shirt. You *can* go wrong with something else.

Your tie should have a conservative pattern. You can read a lot of opinions on what the best tie color is. Some experts say to stay away from red or other bright colors. My personal experience has been that a brightly colored (CONSERVATIVE!) tie looks great with a navy suit and generally produces good results. Whatever you do, don't wear a tie that has anything other than a standard pattern on it. Don't wear one with Looney Tunes characters, airplanes, or Sponge Bob on it. Only wear a tie with a conservative pattern.

Shoes should be dress, black or brown, and made from the skin of a cow. They should be appropriately shined and not scuffed or worn-looking. Boots are not shoes. Black cowboy boots are especially not shoes. Sketchers-style sneaker crossovers are not dress shoes. If you're not exactly sure what I mean by a dress shoe, take a look at the previous example of business attire. Think of something your grandfather would be comfortable wearing to church.

Socks should likewise be dark in color and match your shoes. White or light colored socks are a guaranteed one-way ticket home. When wearing the navy blue, black, or charcoal gray suit, you cannot go wrong with black socks.

Briefcase

There will be a list of documents, photos, etc. that you'll be required to bring with you. Nothing says, "I'm not prepared" more than showing up on Open Day clutching a bunch of paperwork and photographs to your chest in a loose bundle. Put everything you need in a professional-looking case or folder. Anything leather-bound will suffice. Do not carry your documents in a Hello Kitty backpack, or any backpack for that matter. Do not stuff all your paperwork into your pocket and hand it to your assessors in a crumpled heap. For men, a briefcase is a great professional-looking choice, and for women a leather-bound binder or satchel are good options. Ladies, stuffing everything into your tiny, stylish, Dolce & Gabanna purse is not the same thing.

Leave your electronic devices at home

We live in an age of continual connectivity, almost instantaneous information exchange, and huge social networks. Carrying a smart phone on your person at all times is the new normal. We all get that. Nothing will bring your interview, and this opportunity, to a screeching halt faster than a cell phone ringing at the wrong time.

I recommend leaving your phone at home. I know that means you won't be able to tweet your friends the second your assessment if over, but believe me when I say you *can* live without it for a few hours. Here is why you should not even bring it: You can have every good intention of shutting if off for the interview. You can remind yourself *again* that you need to shut if off as you walk in the building. Then things start happening fast. You're meeting people; you're going here, you're going there, and the next thing you know, your ringer is playing "Shine bright like a diamond" for your interviewers. I've seen it happen many, many times. Don't let it happen to you. It's much easier to just leave it.

If you don't have a place to leave it, or there's information on it you *absolutely need* for the interview, make sure you shut the phone off. Tie a string around your finger, put your watch on the other arm, tape the phone to your head, whatever it takes to remind yourself to shut it off. *Setting your phone to vibrate is not the same as shutting it off.* A phone vibrating in a small room with three or four people sitting around a table is just the same as ringing, except that you sit there and pretend it's not really ringing, even though everyone in the room knows it is.

Headphones are also a big issue. I know it's hard to spend any period of downtime not plugged in to something, but it looks bad. Listening to music with headphones on in the middle of a group of others makes you look disengaged and anti-social. Remember, this is a people business. Leave your headphones at home. That way you won't even be tempted.

Dealing with electronic devices is easy: Don't bring them.

Points to remember

- ✓ Women's attire
    - Dark colored knee length skirt suit, wool blend, tailored.
    - White or cream blouse, appropriately buttoned.
    - Dark colored medium heel dress shoes.
    - Stocking should be "nude" and match your skin tone.
    - Hair should be worn neatly, in a bun if possible.
    - Jewelry should be limited to one small earring per ear, a watch, and a wedding ring if married.
    - Light makeup.
    - *Very* light fragrance.
- ✓ Men's attire
    - Dark colored suit, wool blend, tailored.
    - White or light blue shirt.

- Conservative tie with a pattern.
- Dark colored dress shoes, appropriately shined.
- No facial hair.
- No piercings.
- Carry all required documents in a professional case or folder

Grooming

Similar to the strict dress code, personal grooming is an area of considerable focus for cabin crew. You will want to emulate what a typical cabin crew looks like in terms of hairstyle, facial hair (for men, not women), etc. Take a conservative route for everything from makeup application to fragrance to fingernail length. You may have been cultivating a set of nails so long that you've effectively excluded yourself from the manual labor pool, but if you want to have a shot at this job, you'll need to trim them back to a manageable length. Let's look at the standard expectations for men and women:

Male grooming standards

Grooming for men is an extremely important aspect. You want to present yourself as a clean cut, healthy, and hygienic professional. Look at the pictures of the male cabin crew in the promotional videos and print ads. They look like safe bets for your mother-in-law. They look steady, reliable, positive, fit, energetic, and clean. This is how you want to present yourself, and what you must become on Open Day.

Hair should be short on the back and sides. No color, highlights, lowlights, etc. Sideburns should not extend past the mid-level of your ear. Eyebrows, nose, and ears should all be trimmed if necessary. If you've been wearing your hair with purple-highlighted spikes for the past few years and you're struggling with which way to go, print out a picture from the Emirates Web site, take it to a hairdresser, and tell them that is the look you need. For men, sometimes it's easier to just ask your buddy to cut your hair with a pair of clippers in his bathroom before you go out on Friday night, but keep in mind how important a clean, finished look is in this process. You will want to give some money to a professional hairstylist to ensure you have the look you're going for.

Lastly, I know you've been cultivating that goatee for quite a while now. I'm sure everyone loves it, but you must show up to the Open Day with absolutely no facial hair. Not even that scruffy 5'oclock-shadow-beard that looks so sharp. Spend some time in front of the mirror saying your goodbyes, then shave it off.

If you are a fragrance wearer, repeat the phrase, "less is more." People can be extremely sensitive to strong fragrances, and just because you like a particular brand, your assessors may not. Interviewing someone with an overpowering level of fragrance is uncomfortable for the interviewer, and as you can imagine, they don't want someone walking around the back of an airplane for twelve hours that smells like a bottle of cologne exploded on them. If you're going to wear some, *only wear a little.*

Female grooming standards

For ladies, hair should be worn up. The standard for female cabin crew is hair worn in a bun with a cap. You should wear your hair similarly. You don't want it long and flowing. A professional interview appearance is not the same one you'd use for a date. If you have streaks of color in your hair, or your hair color overall is something not found in nature, this is a good time to go back to normal. Braided feathers, beads, anything that doesn't naturally grow out of your head should be removed. Imagine how your grandmother would wear her hair if she were going to church, and you'll want something along those lines. Not very exciting, I know, but you can easily see the standard just by looking on the Emirates Web site. That is the look you are going for.

Makeup application at the company is carefully controlled. There is actually a class on how to properly apply makeup while in uniform. Again, if you look at images of cabin crew at Emirates, they're makeup application is essentially part of the uniform. Try to emulate what you see online: skin colored foundation, vibrant red lipstick. There is not a lot of heavy eye shadow or blush. Think in terms of less is more when applying makeup for your assessment. Fake lashes can reach ridiculous lengths fairly quickly; if you are a fake eyelash wearer, make sure you stick with something short and non-dramatic.

Just like makeup, less is more when applying fragrance. You will be interacting with your assessment team in close quarters. An overpowering amount of fragrance will be considered negative. No one wants to be stuck on an airplane for a long period of time with someone that takes a bath in perfume.

Jewelry

Jewelry is carefully controlled in uniform for both men and women. Women should only wear very conservative earrings, nothing dangly. One small pearl in each ear is a good example. Men should absolutely not wear any earrings.

If you have visible piercings aside from your ears, you will have to remove them. You may think that eyebrow stud that's connected by a chain to your nose ring looks nice with your interview suit, but it will immediately disqualify you. You may also think that no one will notice that barbell in your tongue, but believe me, your assessors will. Just to be clear, because I know people get emotionally attached to their piercings and removing them has ramifications: if you have a piece of metal stuck through a hole in your body that is visible in your interview attire (aside from ears for ladies), take it out.

One ring for men and women is acceptable if you are married. Also, a conservative watch is fine. For women, that means a feminine sized watch made out of metal. For men, also a normal sized watch made of metal, preferably with hands. Do not wear your copy-Movado watch that's the size of a small clock. Something conservative like you would see a banker wearing is the best choice.

Tattoos

This may be a case where that dragon tattoo that stretches from your neck down to the index finger of your left hand can come back to haunt you. Emirates' policy on tattoos is that they cannot be visible in any way while in uniform. Covering a tattoo with makeup or a bandage does not count. By not visible, they mean non-existent. You may be able to hide a tattoo sufficiently to get through the Open Day and even the Assessment Day, but eventually you will have not one but two medical evaluations. One will be in the country of assessment; the other will be upon your arrival in Dubai. If you have a tattoo, no matter how well you've hidden it before, they will find it, eventually.

If you have a tattoo that you're not sure will be acceptable, it's best to disclose it right away. Don't think you can hide that tribal design inside your wrist and make it to Dubai, and then the company will give you the OK. If they find out about an unacceptable tattoo after you arrive in Dubai, they will send you home. Be honest up front and it will save everyone a lot of time and frustration. There is no wiggle-room with this policy, and they will not make any special allowances. The only other option for visible tattoos is removal. While possible, tattoo removal takes time. Depending on the type of tattoo and its location, the removal process can take over a year. If this is something you are considering, it's imperative that you act on it now rather than later.

Fingernails

You're going to be offering your hand to a lot of people over the course of the next few days. Your hands should look presentable. If your nails look like something straight out of a vampire movie, or like you've been running them over a cheese grater, it doesn't send a good first impression.

I did a coaching session for an important interview of my own a while back, and this was one of the major feedback points:

"You've got to do something about those nails," was the general idea.

So I took the coach's advice and actually got a manicure. And you know what? It actually makes a big difference. Most guys think trimming their nails down with a pocketknife anytime they have three minutes of downtime is good enough, but when you're trying to look as professional as possible, a manicure makes a difference.

For ladies, short length nails are important. There is no specific length, but if your saying to yourself, "I wonder if my nails are too long?" then they probably are. Trim them to a length so they don't impede normal work duties.

Color is also important. If you're wondering what color is right, you don't want your interviewers to notice any nail color at all. A gloss or French tips are the best conservative choices for an interview. Bright colors are NOT OK. Designs, jewels, and anything that's not gloss or a French tip are NOT OK.

Points to remember

- ✓ Grooming is an important aspect of presentation. Spend some time looking though the Emirates Web site to get an idea of what the male and female grooming standards are.
- ✓ If you have large visible tattoos, just be honest about them. Your assessors will let you know if they're acceptable or not. The only option may be having it removed. Hiding a tattoo while in uniform is not considered acceptable.
- ✓ Consider getting a manicure for you interview. Ladies nails should be gloss or French tip, no colors, designs, or excessive lengths.

Physique

There is a physical standard the assessors are looking for. There's no way to sugarcoat that. Look at the cabin crew pictures on the Web site and you will get an idea of the average physique for this position. If your height/weight ratio is significantly different than what you see there, it's not the end of the world, but it is something you will have to change before you can seriously compete for this job. The physical reach requirement is 212cm. An important distinction to make is this is *not* a height requirement: it's a reach requisite. You may be on the shorter side, but if you have long arms and can touch a marker at 212cm on your tippy toes, then you meet the minimum standard for Emirates. There is no point going down this road if you cannot, as the company will not budge on this due to regulatory requirements.

If you have several weeks before Open Day, you can actually make significant progress toward this standard by changing your diet and exercise level, probably more than you would consider possible right now. There is no better motivation for improving your health and fitness level than having a clear goal to work toward. Getting a cabin crew position is as good a goal as any.

Before you make a major change in your life and modify your diet and exercise level, consult with a physician. Then, if you really want to see significant results in a short period of time, set up a program with a personal trainer. Give them a clear idea of your goal, and your timeframe, and they will help you reach that goal by the assessment date. Paying professionals to help you isn't cheap, but as with your interview suit, think of this as an investment in your future. You can't get the job without a nice suit, and you can't get this job if you don't fit down the aisle.

Body shaping underwear has been gaining popularity recently. It's basically tight spandex that fits under your clothes and helps put curves in the right places, while taking them out of the wrong ones. Wait a minute! Can I just buy some spandex underwear and then lace up a corset so tightly I start seeing stars? You could, but keep in mind that you will undergo two physicals (see chapter 12): one in your home country and one when you arrive in Dubai. If you look like a completely different person when you strip these garments off, there may be an issue. It's better (and healthier) to make the change through diet and exercise than trying to pull one over on them.

How to Pass the Emirates Cabin Crew Interview

Points to remember

✓ You will be evaluated on whether you physically match the standard the company is looking for. If you have enough time, then you can make significant progress toward meeting this standard.

Selling yourself: actions speak (MUCH!) louder than words

Body language

I hope I've driven home the importance of making a solid first impression, and the way you are dressed is a huge component to that equation. Your assessors on Open Day will see you walking up to their table in your smart and professional business attire. They will begin to form an opinion in the few steps it takes you to present yourself in front of them.

If you are diligent about the issues we've covered so far, that first opinion when they see you will be, "this looks promising."

And that is perfect. If that is your starting point, you are exactly where you want to be.

Here is a secret about interviewers: they either work for you or against you. There's no middle ground. If they like what they see initially, then they will build a case to hire you. If they don't like what they see, then they look for a reason to dismiss you. It's human nature, and it's *that* simple. This is why your first impression is so important.

How to Pass the Emirates Cabin Crew Interview

You can't get the job solely based on a strong first impression. On the outside, you can look like the most perfect cabin crew candidate ever, but if you fail to demonstrate any measurable social tact, all your first impression effort has been wasted. There has to be some substance under the appearance.

The remaining component to being successful, equally important to how you look, is how you act. Visual presentation is critically important, but so is how you talk, how you walk, how you meet someone, etc. All of these qualities and more are communicated non-verbally (whether you know it or not, and now you do!) through body language. Body language is the second major contributor to the first and lasting impression you will make.

If I asked you how human beings communicate, chances are that you would say with words, which is true to a certain degree. While we do communicate with one another verbally, there is an incredible amount of information that in conveyed non-verbally, and this is what we refer to as body language. Some experts estimate that up to 93% of human communication happens through body language. If we put that together with how long we have to make a positive first impression in an interview, which is around four seconds, that tells that you that how you look, how you act, and how you carry yourself are significant factors in how you will be judged. And that judgment happens very quickly.

While the evaluation is continuous, there are three critical times where you body language will be scrutinized the closest:

- ✓ Walking toward (and away) from your evaluators, such as during the approach for the CV handover, or the one-on-one interview.
- ✓ When you meet for the first time and you introduce yourself, then again at the end of a meeting when the meeting comes to a close. This can happen very quickly, when you meet to hand over your CV, or there can be a long time in between. Don't forget the closing is just as important as the opening.
- ✓ The actual interaction with your assessors, both seated and standing.

At each of these junctures, your assessors will be (both consciously and sub-consciously) paying very close attention to the non-verbal signals that you are sending out. You may be saying how friendly, confident, and professional you are, but if the signals you send don't agree with the words coming out of your mouth, then what you're saying won't matter.

There are five critical components to body language that you must master if you want to send the right impression and get the job. They are *not* ranked in order of importance in the following list. Each one is just as important as the other. The five critical components are:

1. Eye Contact
2. Smile
3. Handshake
4. Personal Space
5. General bearing

At the end of this section, we'll talk about how to practice these components so that when Open Day comes around, you have them down pat. For now, I'd like you to start by just being conscious of these components and how you implement them in your day-to-day interactions with other. Pay attention to your eye contact when talking with your friends versus talking with a stranger. Make a note of whether you smile to the barista behind the counter when you order a coffee. Take a snapshot of how you are carrying yourself when you enter a room full of strangers. This self-evaluation period is very important: you need to have an idea of what you are doing well, and what you need to work on to perform at your peak on Open Day. You cannot fix your performance if you don't know what's broken, so really devote some time to introspection of these components. With that being said, let's expand on them.

Eye contact

Eye contact is where people new to interviewing have the most trouble. Failing to maintain good eye contact can result in looking insecure, and won't allow you to establish any type of relationship with your assessors. If you ever take the time to watch friendly, outgoing people interact, they maintain a high level of eye contact throughout their conversations. It helps them establish a rapport with others. That is exactly what you want to do during the assessment, and as cabin crew in general. The handshake sends a nearly instantaneous first impression, and we're going to say a few (much more than a few, actually) words on that shortly. For now, I'd like you to think of eye contact as a handshake that occurs over a much longer period of time. If a handshake is like a sprint that takes a few seconds, then eye contact is a marathon and lasts the duration of your interview experience. You must maintain the pace of your eye for the entire interview.

Eye contact in an interview is a good thing, but like with almost anything in life it is possible to over-do eye contact and have too much of a good thing. The trick is doing it just right. Looking a person in the eyes acknowledges your interest and involvement in the conversation. Prolonged, uninterrupted eye contact, however, can be construed as a sign of aggression. This is why, in a normal conversation, the participants break eye contact momentarily every few seconds and then re-establish it. A good technique to give a detailed answer without being too intense is to shift your eye contact between each eye and the center of the eyebrows. This prevents the death stare effect that many serial killers are fond of. If you notice that you have a tendency to stare at people unblinking for long periods of time, correct it. You may be coming off a bit like a creepy lunatic.

Being insecure about performance will really come out in an applicant's eye contact. Specifically, if they are unsure of how they're going to perform, you will typically see them talking to their hands, the floor, or even to no one in particular off to the side of the room. This is what you must absolutely, positively avoid.

Maintaining eye contact with someone during conversation is a standard common courtesy, and you probably do it without even noticing you are. The interview process isn't your standard conversation, however. There are some specific aspects to consider while interviewing: Maintaining eye contact with someone that asks you pointed questions can be difficult. If the person asking you these questions isn't particularly friendly (and there's no guarantee they will be), it can be even *more* difficult. There will be times that you need to pause and think through your answers. These are just a couple of examples of time you'll need to be aware of what's going on with your eye contact, because you may want to look down or away during an uncomfortable situation. You have to resist that urge and maintain normal level of eye contact at all times.

I personally experienced a challenging eye contact situation during a panel interview. We were all sitting around a table, with each person on the panel looking at me intently. They went around the table and took turns asking their respective questions. In a panel interview setting there is a tendency for the interviewee to only look at and answer the interviewer asking the question. You need to make sure to include everyone in the room in all of your answers. In a panel interview setting, and specifically in the group dynamic exercises we'll discuss later, you'll need to make an effort to include each member in attendance. Shift your eye contact from one person to the next each time you make a statement or ask a question. Even if the people in the group around you aren't looking at you, they may be looking down or writing something, keep attempting to establish eye contact with everyone. The only exception to this rule is for short, one or two word answers. If you are asked a question and the answer only consists of a few words, it's acceptable to just maintain eye contact with the individual posing the question.

As you're answering questions and maintaining eye contact, at some point you'll be asked a question that requires some contemplation. Where should you look while you're thinking? Anytime there's a pause and you have to think, try to look up. Looking up gives the impression that you're being genuine and truthful. Looking down gives the impression that you're being evasive and deceitful. In the vast majority of interviews I've done, I eventually ask a question about something in the applicant's past they weren't proud of: a goal they hadn't achieved, a time they'd gotten in trouble at school, a bad grade they're received, etc. Every time someone answered a question along these lines and they had a hard time maintaining eye contact, I got the impression that they were not being completely honest. Constantly shifting your eyes around the room sends an impression of being nervous and evasive.

Here's another example. Have you ever seen a child get in trouble for misbehaving? The next time you have the opportunity to witness it, or if you just want to run out and start yelling at some random kid in the street, pay careful attention to their eyes.

I walked into the bathroom not too long ago and found my son giving the dog a bath in the toilet. -SIGH- This was a recurring issue. I know that *he* knows that dogs don't go in toilets (unless maybe they're on fire, but that's another story, altogether). I told him, "No," and asked him why he was giving the dog a bath in the toilet. Again. He then produced a long and extremely detailed narrative, which you had to be a writer to really appreciate. There were a lot of complex aspects to the story, but the main point was that the dog actually "told" my son she needed a bath in the toilet. Guess where he looked the entire time he told the story? He looked down at the floor, then over at the corner, then back at the floor. He looked everywhere he could to not meet my eyes.

Grownups can have a tendency to do the exact same thing. Being nervous can also make you revert to this behavior. Believe me when I say that if you're interviewing for a job you really want, the butterflies will be fluttering in your stomach and you'll be nervous. If you haven't worked on maintaining good eye contact before the interview, being nervous can cause you to shift your gaze around without knowing it, and that's not the impression you want to leave on your assessors. Practice, practice, practice.

How to Pass the Emirates Cabin Crew Interview

Points to remember

✓ It's imperative to maintain good eye contact with everyone you are interacting with. DO NOT look down while speaking, talk to your hands, or fail to establish eye contact with everyone person you interact with.

Smile

Look at those billboards, magazine ads, and Web sites for Emirates...if you can find a member of the cabin crew that is *NOT* smiling, let me know and I will (literally) eat my own shoe. All the cabin crew members in those pictures have a vibrant smile. This is a clear example of the image cabin crew are expected to present. Since this is the job you want, it's the image *you* are expected to present.

Smile, smile, and smile. You should be smiling throughout the entirety of your assessment. A little personality goes a long way, and nothing sends the message better than a great smile. You need your assessors to remember you as a smiling, upbeat applicant.

Here's a test: look in a mirror and act like you're meeting yourself for the first time. Do it first without smiling, and see how it looks. Now introduce yourself to yourself again, only this time do it with a big, beaming smile on your face. Which one looks better? Which person would you be more inclined to hire?

Here's another test you can do: the next time you're ordering a coffee or a meal in a restaurant, give the server a great big smile and ask how they're doing before placing your order. I bet they will respond in kind. Later, make an order to another server but with a serious, intense look on your face. I bet their response will be much different. Everyone enjoys dealing with a friendly person. Show your assessors how friendly and outgoing you are with your brilliant smile. If you find yourself at any time during the assessment process *NOT* smiling, correct the situation immediately.

Combining a winning smile with good eye contact is a critical aspect of successfully attaining a cabin crew position. You will be judged on how you look, how you carry yourself, and how you interact with others. If that fact makes you uncomfortable, then you need to come to terms with it or this may not be the position for you. Remember, once you are hired, you are a walking, talking representation of Emirates. The company has very high standards and you will be expected to maintain them. You will continually be judged throughout your assessment on how you present yourself.

Handshake

A good handshake is an incredibly important part of the overall impression. It sends an instantaneous impression, and many times is the only physical interaction you will have with your assessors. A good, solid handshake can work considerably to your advantage. A weak one can almost single-handedly (Ha! Single-handed, get it?) derail your entire interview.

A weak handshake is one of my personal pet peeves. There is nothing that sends a worse impression than a cold, limp handshake. It feels like someone is offering you a dead fish to grab hold of. I've spoken to many people in hiring, inside and outside aviation, and there is a unanimous consensus: anyone that can't muster the enthusiasm to give a good handshake is not an employment risk worth taking.

What constitutes a good handshake? First, let's talk about position: square your shoulders to the person you're meeting and hold your hand out straight in front of you with your thumb pointed at the ceiling. DO NOT twist your body as you offer your hand, resulting in one shoulder being ahead of the other. That implies informality. DO NOT turn your hand sideways. Offering a handshake with the back of your hand toward the ceiling implies dominance. Offering your hand with the palm up implies submissiveness. Square shoulders, open hand, thumb up is the goal.

Three grip levels are available to you: limp, bone crusher, and normal. My recommendation is to apply the normal grip level. A limp handshake is one where the hand dangles lifelessly and no pressure is applied during the handshake process. A limp handshake implies submissiveness, lack of confidence, or both. Being the recipient of a limp handshake leaves me with a general dirty feeling, followed by the need to take a hot shower and wash the entire experience away. A bone crusher, on the other hand, is when the applicant tries to quantify his/her desire for the job through the strength of their grip. This can signify either dominance or insecurity, and in extreme cases can be uncomfortable for the interviewer. Again, not the impression you're going for.

A normal handshake grip is similar to what you use to carry an umbrella or your briefcase. The web of your hand, the area between your thumb and forefinger, should meet the web of your interviewer's. Apply your grip to the interviewers hand itself, don't just grab their fingers or use only your thumb to apply pressure. Release the handshake before the end of your interviewer's introduction; usually about one to three pumps, if you need a number.

How to Pass the Emirates Cabin Crew Interview

If your hands tend to be cold, put them in your pocket to warm them up prior to the introduction. If you have clammy hands, casually wipe your palm again your pant leg or skirt as you raise your hand so you can offer a dry, warm hand for the shaking.

Grab a friend or family member and practice your handshake a couple of times. If you see them wincing in pain, or they snatch their hand back and cradle it in terror, then you'll want to adjust your technique. Eventually, you'll get to the point where you're comfortable giving a consistently good handshake, and you can move on to bigger and better things.

Points to remember

✓ Handshakes are critically important to sending positive impressions. If you are not used to shaking hands or not comfortable doing so, start practicing.

Personal space

Here's a big scientific word: proxemics. That's a fancy word for the study of measurable distances between people when they meet. I like to simplify things whenever possible, so I just call it the personal space bubble. Everyone maintains a certain bubble of space around their person that they consider theirs. Your cultural upbringing, the setting you're in, and the participants involved generally dictate the size of that bubble. In North America and Europe, a person's personal space bubble is about two feet around them. People raised in these cultures reserve anything inside that two foot bubble for intimate acquaintances.

Continually encroaching into what someone considers their personal space bubble can give an impression of being too familiar or pushy. Standing too far from someone's bubble can give the impression of being cool or standoffish. Neither of these impressions is the one you want to give.

How to Pass the Emirates Cabin Crew Interview

In the interview setting, when you're meeting and greeting, you want to be between two and four feet from the person or people that you're interacting with. Anything inside that two foot bubble and you'll run the risk of making your interviewer uncomfortable. Violating their culturally allotted personal space bubble isn't a good way to start the day.

If you're having a hard time consistently judging the distance to stand from someone, especially when it's a departure from how you've grown up, try this:

Use a piece of tape to make a mark on the floor two feet from a mirror. Practice walking up to the mirror and saying hello. Do this several times over a couple of days. You'll get a good feel for the right distance to stand without invading someone's personal space or acting like you're being introduced to a plague carrier.

The position you're interviewing for involves dealing directly with the public in close confines and limited space. Some cultures have developed a norm of wearing hygiene masks while surrounded by large groups of people. This is definitely not the impression you want to give. Hygiene masks are not part of the product Emirates is selling, so if this is something you typically do, leave the mask home for the entire process. This includes checking into the hotel.

Points to remember

✓ Different cultures have different standards for personal space. Maintain a two to four foot personal space bubble in the assessment setting.

General bearing

Just to re-emphasize: your interview begins from the time you walk into the building for the Open Day event. While walking or standing, make sure that you are standing straight with your shoulders slightly back. Avoid fidgeting, playing with your hands, twirling your hair, and any other exaggerated or nervous movements while you're waiting. One common reaction many people have to stressful environments are bouncing their legs or moving them constantly in some way. Be conscious of this and refrain from doing so during the entire process.

When you meet and are introduced to people, square your shoulders to them and stand up straight. If you ever have the opportunity to observe screening events like this, you can instantly pick out applicants that are going to do well just by how they stand. They personify confidence and self-assurance, and this is exactly what the HR representatives are looking for. You can't look confident and self-assured if you're subconsciously shrinking away from people every time you meet with them.

I know what you're thinking: "I would never do that."

As I sit here and write this, I am telling you that people who are insecure about their performance do exactly that. When you are practicing your interaction before the Open Day, and then when you get to Open Day, make sure your shoulders are square with whomever you're interacting with, and that you're standing up straight at all times.

As you advance through the process, you'll eventually interact with people while seated at a table. This occurs both during the group dynamic exercises and personal interviews. Make sure you sit like you stand, straight up, with shoulders slightly back, squarely facing the people with whom you're interacting. Do not lean forward in your chair or slouch back. Both of these actions have negative associations. Keep your feet flat on the floor and avoid fidgeting, bouncing a leg, swinging your knees back and forth, or any other repetitive movements. Crossing your legs and placing an ankle on your knee while seated is considered a very defensive and guarded position. If this is a position you typically sit in and find comfortable, you'll want to avoid it. Keep both feet flat on the floor at all times, except when walking.

Be conscious of what is going on with your head. I don't mean inside it (but that's important, too!), but be aware of how you're holding it during interactions. Your head should be kept level any time that you are talking with anyone during the assessment process. When you are listening to someone, particularly if involved in an individual conversation, tilting your head *slightly* indicates being receptive and attentive. Aside from that, keep your head in a level position

Some people have a tendency to talk with their hands. Gesturing with your hands *slightly* while you speak isn't necessarily a bad thing, and can be effective when you want to emphasize a point. Don't get *too* animated, however, or it starts to detract from your performance. Imagine there is a one-foot by one-foot box in front of you. If you use your hands when you talk, keep them in this box. Any hand movements outside the 1x1 box and it can affect your credibility.

You'll generally want to fold your hands and put them in your lap. In an interview setting, I keep my hands in my lap because if I place them on the table, then I have a tendency to clench them together and hunch forward, which can send an overly aggressive impression. If you do place your hands on the table, fold them in front of you and continue sitting straight.

One unconscious mannerism that can signal deception is when a person touches their face, ear, or nose while speaking. Adhere to the

1x1 box rule, and you won't have a problem. Under no circumstances should you raise your hands above shoulder level *at any point* during the interview, unless your hair has actually caught on fire.

A hand gesture that conveys openness and honesty is showing your palms while speaking. If you gesture with your hands, position your palms up whenever possible. Avoid pointing directly at someone, and avoid clenching your hands in fists while speaking or listening.

Points to remember

✓ Posture and the way you carry yourself are important presentation aspects. Sit professionally at tables at all times, and don't make large or fast gestures with your hands while speaking.

Mind your surroundings

This is a critical concept to understand: Your face-to-face interview does *NOT* begin when you finally get to meet with the assessment team. Your interview beings when you walk through the door!

I have conducted a lot of interviews for aviation companies. I can't even count the number of applicants that have lost jobs because they acted inappropriately when they thought no one was looking. The entire

Open and Assessment Days are your interviews. Do you think no one is looking while you're milling around in line, waiting for your turn? Could a member from the HR team be using the restroom at the same time you and your friends are?

They are most definitely looking at you. I guarantee it. That's what this whole process is all about: you being looked at and evaluated. Don't make the mistake of thinking it's not happening every second of each day.

That stranger that walks up to you and starts a conversation: are they an applicant or part of the assessment team? Could be either one. It's not unusual for companies to circulate someone in the crowd to interact with applicants. Treat every single person you meet like they are interviewing you. If you act like you are being interviewed at all times, even when you step into the restroom, then you will never be caught unawares.

Two quick examples to illustrate my point:

1. Applicants were waiting in a lobby for their turn to be called back for a one-on-one interview. While they were waiting, two applicants (who apparently knew each other beforehand) started having a casual conversation. While they waited, the conversation continued, grew louder, and soon they were telling jokes, using profanity, and

basically acting unprofessionally. Members of the interview team, who the applicants didn't realize were watching them, noted this behavior. Their interviews were extremely short and ended with the predictable result.

2. I was walking into a building to interview a group of applicants. It was raining and I was carrying an armload of paperwork for the day's interviews (not taking my own advice and carrying a briefcase, apparently). A gentleman hurried past me on the sidewalk, wearing a suit, also trying to get out of the rain. Judging from his attire, he was one of the applicants I would be interviewing that day. He pulled open the door and ran inside to get out of the rain, letting the door slam in my face without even looking back. Not a great first impression. If he had simply been more conscious and courteous, and held the door for one second, my impression of him would have been totally different.

You never know with whom you're meeting, or who is watching at any given time. Don't let your guard down, even for a second. Maybe you're staying in the same hotel as the HR team, so don't forget to consider that group of people sitting next to you in the bar may be doing your interview the next morning.

Mind your surroundings at all times. Remember, every second of the day, from the time you walk through the door until you walk out again, is your interview.

Points to remember

✓ Keep in mind where you are and what you are doing. If you think you are not being observed and evaluated at all times, you are wrong.

✓ Your interview begins from the time you walk through the door of the building until you walk out again.

Practice makes perfect

A significant number of applicants at Open Days are screened out based on this initial first impression. If you don't actively practice the many aspects of good first impressions we've gone over so far, you performance on Open Day will suffer. Talking (or reading in this case) and doing are two very different things. One of the most important secrets to making a good first impression is *practice*. I could write a list of 1000 points to remember to make a good first impression, but if you don't go out there and actually put these points into practice in your daily activities, they won't help.

How to Pass the Emirates Cabin Crew Interview

Think about a professional tennis player. Do you suppose he just wakes up one morning and competes at Wimbledon? Absolutely not. He practices and practices so that when he does compete in the big match, he is prepared. Interviewing effectively is no different, and this interview is equivalent to winning at Wimbledon. If you never *physically* practice the techniques we talk about, and just assume it will all come together on Open Day, you will be disappointed. Going over an answer to an interview question in your head is not the same as speaking it. You'll be surprised how difficult it can be translating thoughts into words when you're answering questions. The more you practice, the easier it will become.

How do you practice for an interview without doing one? It can be as easy as sitting down in a chair and verbally introducing yourself while you're alone in a room. You can get a friend and practice walking into a room and shaking their hand, or you can practice simply sitting at a table in a professional manner (more on that later). Each of these examples sounds basic and easy, but I absolutely 100% guarantee that it's not so easy when someone is staring at you trying to decide if you should have one of the most sought-after jobs in the world.

Here's a personal example: I had an interview scheduled with one of the top airlines in the world. I thought I would just go in...have a casual chat…and walk out with the job. What I didn't realize was that when I sat down in front of the three people interviewing me, I was really, really nervous. I also didn't realize (until halfway through my interview) that I was swinging my legs back and forth on the swivel chair I was sitting on. I noticed that I was stuttering and saying, "uh" a lot. An awful lot. All those problems manifested themselves because I hadn't prepared or practiced for this interview that was hugely competitive. I didn't get the job, but I learned a lot of things about what not to do in an interview. It was a very expensive lesson, as I never got another opportunity at that job. Don't make the same mistake I did. Practice.

It is vitally important for you to be able to see yourself from a third-person perspective in your practice sessions. You may be surprised how you perform when observed by someone else, compared to how you *think* you are performing. You'll notice a nervous habit you didn't know you had, or the fact that every third word you say is "um". It's easy to correct nervous behavior if you're aware of it, and that's why you need to take a look at yourself.

Grab a video recorder, have someone record you with your phone, or at the very least find a full-length mirror. You need to practice walking into a room, greeting people (just greet yourself in the mirror), and smiling. Study how you look and how you're conducting yourself from someone else's perspective. What can you improve on? Are you presenting yourself the way a cabin crew member at a premier airline would? You won't know until you can observe yourself firsthand. Put on your interview suit or dress. See how you look in it when you enter the room. Make sure it's comfortable and you don't mind wearing it for a long period of time. If you simply take some time and practice presenting yourself, you'll be far ahead of the majority of applicants on both Open and Assessment Days.

Points to remember

- ✓ Practice, practice, practice. In order to perform your best, you have to work on perfecting your skills.
- ✓ Find a way to record and view yourself in an interview setting, work getting rid of nervous habits or unconfident behavior.

Physical requirements

Unfortunately, you can't just plop down in a first class seat with the passengers while you're flying between Dubai and Sydney, order a drink, and watch the world fly by. You will have to actually work, and there are physical requirements associated with the duties that you'll have to perform. You will be pushing heavy food and beverage carts up and down the aisles. You will need to place and reach items in overhead bins. On occasion, you'll be helping that little old lady hoist her bag (that weighs more than she does!) into the overhead compartment.

You will need to access and use emergency equipment such as defibrillators, oxygen bottles, fire extinguishers, etc. You will be trained in the use of all this equipment and more, and you must be able to physically manage using it. You'll receive open water training where you will simulate a water landing and have to get yourself, your fellow crew members, and conscious or unconscious passengers into a life raft.

For all these reasons, while you are being evaluated on how professionally you meet, greet, and interact with others, you are also being evaluated on your physical capabilities.

There is a reach requirement of 212cm without heels. The HR team will bring a calibrated device and you WILL be given a reach test. While you can't necessarily fake it if you don't make the height requirement, you can stand on your tippy toes during the assessment. If you are right on the line, give yourself of boost and it may be enough to get you to the limit.

Part II: The Emirates Interview

Everything we've talked about up to this point has been more or less general, meaning that it's good technique to use in any business professional, competitive interview. Now we'll look at how the specific process for becoming a cabin crewmember in the United Arab Emirates works. The order of events changes slightly depending on geographic location, venue, and that number of attendees, and the event may occur all on one day or over several. The screening process, regardless of length, consists of the following elements:

- ✓ Fill out the online application. Even if you'll be attending an Open Day that's available to walk-ins off the street, it's best to fill out the application online before the event.
- ✓ Attend an Open Day event. This event varies depending by country. Sometimes it's open to walk-ins, other times you must register in advance to attend. Check the Web site for Open Day information at

a location near you. *By the way, this is also a punctuality test*: if you're not in the ballroom by the published start time, you're out for good.

- ✓ You'll be issued a sticker upon check-in for the Open Day, which you'll wear for the duration of the event
- ✓ Once everyone has been assembled for the day, you'll view a promotional video about Emirates.
- ✓ A representative from Human Resources will give a briefing on what to expect from a career at Emirates and life in Dubai.
- ✓ The floor will be opened for questions from the applicants.
- ✓ Following applicant questions, the first major screening event occurs: the Resume Handover. Several tables will be set up at the head of the room and you will submit your resume to the appropriate location based on the number you've been issued.
- ✓ There will be a break for lunch, and only applicants that have passed the resume handover screening will return for further events. *Note:* have limited to no interaction with the HR people for the resume handover--the entire screening event is based on your personal presentation and that of the resume you hand in. *It's all about first impressions here!*
- ✓ The first group dynamic exercise takes place. Applicants are split into groups of approximately 20-25. Following this event, applicants

are informed whether they will continue on with the process.
- ✓ Applicants participate in the second group dynamic in smaller groups of around 8-10. A more complex scenario is presented. Following this event, applicants are informed who will be continuing.
- ✓ English comprehension test.
- ✓ Aptitude test. Applicants are informed who will continue.
- ✓ One-on-one interview with a member from the human resource staff.
- ✓ Generally a minimum of fourteen day waiting period for notification to come in the mail. Many have waited up to six weeks for notification and being accepted.

That is a general summary of the process. Think of each step along the way as a gate. You have to pass through each gate in succession to secure the cabin crew job waiting for you at the end. Failing to give your top performance in any given phase is all it takes to miss the opportunity. That is why it's so important to get everything right the first time, and why it's a good idea that your reading this book and preparing beforehand.

This will sound harsh, but it is true, and it's important that you understand the reality: Emirates has absolutely nothing invested in you. There are literally hundreds of people standing in line behind you trying to get this job. That's just at the Open Day you're attending. If you look at all the Open Days around the world, you're competing with thousands of similarly qualified applicants. Attention to detail during this entire process is paramount.

If your interviewers see *one thing* they don't like, *just one*, their view is, "why take the risk?" and they move on to the next applicant. That may sound discouraging, initially, but now that fact will work to your advantage. This is why: because you are reading this book. The majority of applicants that show up to Open Day are unprepared, the vast majority. They don't understand how competitive this process is. They don't know how important it is to have the application completed correctly, or even to have it completed, at all. They will show up thinking they will improvise, wing it, and everything will work out. But they won't be dressed right, they won't act right, they won't present right, and that is why the majority of applicants are rejected. You will understand the importance of every small detail in this process (or I haven't done a very good job of emphasizing it!!!), and thus you will stand out for the right reasons.

Video and QA

When you enter the hotel for your interview, you will be added to the list of attendees and issued a sticker with a number to be worn at all times. This number is how you will be identified throughout the process, so make sure you know it and listen for it. Nothing annoys interviewers like calling out, "Number 24!" repeatedly, only to have you stare blankly at them for several minutes before realizing you, in fact, are number 24.

You will view a promotional video put together by Emirates giving a synopsis on what you can expect from a position as a cabin crew member. Next, an HR representative will come forward and give you a briefing, elaborating more on the points made in the video. This whole process is partly informational, partly sales pitch. This is a good job, don't get me wrong, but after you see the view and listen to HR, they will have you convinced it's the best job in the world. And maybe it is. If you were lukewarm on whether this was the right thing or not, you will now desperately want to be successful. Which is exactly what they want.

After the video and presentation, they will open up the floor for "Question time." Sounds harmless. Is this a friendly no harm, no foul, free question session where you can ask anything that springs to your mind? What do you think? The evaluation began the second you walked through the door. This is part of the process.

Those who ask questions will be noted by HR. That's not necessarily a bad thing, but it is something to be aware of. If you have a legitimate, well-thought out question that wasn't answered by either of the previous presentations, this is a good time to ask. Just be smart about what you ask.

You may have heard the term, "There are no stupid questions."

That is not entirely accurate. Let's say the video talks about, for example, what your compensation will be if you get the job. Then the HR rep talks about what your compensation will be during their presentation. If you raise your hand and ask what your compensation is going to be, that is a stupid question. They have already covered that twice. Odds are, they will make a note next to your number on their list.

Seems overly simplistic, right? Who would ask a question that's already been covered? It happens like this:

In the days leading up to your Open Day, you're trying to come up with an intelligent, well-spoken question that you can ask so you'll be noticed right away.

Then it pops into your head, "I know, I can ask how much we're going to be paid!"

All through the video and the HR rep's speech, all you're doing is going over and over that question in your head. How you're going to raise your hand, intelligently phrase it, etc. You're so fixated on your question that you don't really notice that it gets answered, maybe even a couple of times. Finally, it's your chance and you raise your hand and ask (because you've been saving this great question up all this time), and the HR people wonder why you didn't understand this when they covered compensation earlier.

The moral of the story is: if you have a legitimate question, then by all means ask it, but don't ask a question just to ask a question. Everyone in the room will be looked at and evaluated at some point. Don't be in a rush to have the spotlight shine on you. You'll have plenty of time for that later.

If you do have a legitimate question (and it hasn't been covered!), remember what we talked about with first impressions, because you are making yours. Practice verbalizing your question--there is no substitute. The first time that I had to stand in front of a room full of people and speak, it felt like I was talking with a mouth full of peanut butter. Nothing would come out right. Speaking in front of a large gathering of people, where they are all focused on you, is very different than speaking to a small number of people. Make sure you've practiced saying your question beforehand or it won't come out quite as neatly as it sounds in your head. Never forget the Golden Rule to public speaking: SLOW MOTION. Its sounds silly, but believe me, I have watched stumbles many times, and the common denominator is too much speed. Practice speaking slowly to your peers as Open Day approaches. You will be more articulate with a slower pace because your mind is now working at a manageable level. You will come across as more confident and controlled; in effect, you will own the moment. You will be surprised how quickly (no pun intended) you will see results. This is one of the gems to advancement, as it will assist you at every stage onwards in the process, and life in general.

Points to remember

- ✓ You can and should ask a question if you have one, but don't ask a question just to ask a question.
- ✓ Make sure you speak clearly and intelligently if you ask something. You are now making your first impression.
- ✓ Don't forget – slow it down. You're not an auctioneer, speak clearly and take your time.

The resume handover

Following the Q and A session, there will be a short coffee break. During this pause, the HR team will set up several tables at the head of the meeting room. Each table will be manned by one member of the HR team, and applicants will be invited to line up at the applicable table based on the number you were issued at the beginning of the day. Table 1 will service numbers 100-200, table 2 200-300, so on and so forth.

This is the first major screening event of the day. You can see from the numbers involved (one person screening at least 100 applicants) that they must move quickly through the crowd. The HR rep at your table will give you a quick greeting, take your resume, and then mark it yes or no based on that brief twenty second exchange.

You can't say a whole lot in twenty seconds, so what do you think that majority of this particular screen is based on? This is all about first impressions. Does this applicant have the potential to fit into the Emirates mold? That's all the HR reps are looking for. Anyone that is outside the acceptable norm is weeded out. They will be screening out more than they will be accepting at this stage. If you have taken to heart all the previous sections, you <u>will</u> fall within the acceptable norm. Just remember: *each part of the first impression is equally as important as the others.* Attire, grooming, smiling, handshake, eye contact, general bearing--this is the point you need to bring it all into focus. You have to present the total package in twenty seconds, and giving a great first impression by putting everything together is the only way to do that.

Following the resume handover, there will be a break, and applicants will be notified whether they will be continuing on to the Group Dynamic.

Remember names

This small but important point applies not only to the resume handover, but all the remaining events of the interview process. Using names in an interview setting is a valuable tool, and one that is undervalued and underutilized by most applicants. You need to try to establish some kind of connection/rapport with your interviewers, and there is no better way than by using their name.

I'd like you to take a moment, and mentally put yourself in the position of an HR representative working at this Open Day event. They are literally meeting hundreds of people at a typical screening. It is a welcome departure from the norm when an applicant actually says hello and goodbye, taking the time and interest to use your name. HR reps are people just like you, and they like it when someone shows some actual interest in them, instead of just viewing them as an obstacle that must be overcome to achieve a cabin crew position. They will have a nametag on, so when you say hello, thank you, and good-bye, make sure you use their name clearly.

You don't have a whole lot of time to interact. A statement to establish a minimal connection can be as simple as, "Samantha, thank you for taking the time to look at my resume. I hope you get some time in your busy schedule to see our beautiful city."

There is no better way to engage someone in a conversation that by using their name. During the group dynamic exercises and when closing your interview are great times to interject people's names and show that you've taken the time to learn theirs. I'm personally terrible at remembering names, so I will typically try to come up with some kind of reminder when I'm introduced to someone:

Leslie has long hair.

Mr. Brown has brown shoes.

Caitlyn's parents couldn't decide between Kate and Lynn.

You get the idea. It doesn't have to make sense; it can even be a rhyme that's nothing more than gibberish:

Mr. Kattenbower took the whole hour.

You may be a great name person, and if you are, then that's perfect. If you're not, and you don't make a point of remembering, by the time you get to the end of your interview, you're going to try to remember you interviewer's name and there will be a great big blank spot there.

It's nice to be able to close your interview with something like, "thanks for taking the time to meet with me, Ms. James (James, like Jessie James the outlaw). I appreciate the opportunity to come here today."

If you don't commit names to memory, then you won't be able to establish that momentary connection that says that you care enough about this process to remember who you're meeting.

Points to remember

- ✓ The Resume Handover is where all this preparation needs to come together. You have as little as twenty seconds to make an impression; it needs to be a good one.
- ✓ Names are important. Make a point of remembering them and interject them anytime it's appropriate.

First group dynamic

After the Resume Handover, there will be a break and applicants continuing in the process will be divided into large groups of anywhere between ten to twenty applicants. Your first group exercise will then begin.

Before we talk about the specifics of this group dynamic in particular, what is a group dynamic? What is the point of the whole exercise?

A group exercise like this puts a bunch of strangers together and forces them to work collectively toward a solution to a problem. The problem, and the solution, interestingly, are mostly irrelevant. What is important, and what the observers are taking notes on, is *how* the group works through the problem. *How* it arrives at its solution. The solution is usually a very subjective one, meaning it's based on opinions, and there is no right or wrong answer.

It's a commonly accepted theory that groups formed for this purpose go through four stages of evolution: forming, storming, norming, and performing. Typically these stages take place over a long period of time with work and professional groups, but since this exercise is time-compressed, they happen fairly quickly. The names of the stages aren't important; you're not going to be quizzed on those later. What is important is what happens during each of these stages of group formation. It's helpful to have an understanding of how a group works to be an effective member and show you can work well with strangers.

Stages of group dynamics are:

- ✓ *Forming*: The group meets, and no one is sure exactly what their role is. A tremendous amount of body language and non-verbal communication occurs during this stage, which is easy for the HR reps to observe. Group members will begin establishing their roles as leaders, contributing members, or followers.
- ✓ *Storming*: The hierarchy of group members forms as verbal communication between members begins. Leaders step forward, wallflowers step back, and members begin to add their contributions. In groups without strong leadership, mediocrity in discussions is supported. Keep in mind that this isn't necessarily a good or bad thing, we're still talking about what happens in general terms.
- ✓ *Norming*: As members settle into their respective roles, progress beings toward finding a solution to the problem. Strong (possibly overbearing) leaders will drive the group toward their solution if input from other members is lacking. Members who contribute little or

nothing toward the solution will become apparent. If a group has good chemistry and works well together, it will be obvious. Similarly, if a group is dysfunctional or not working together effectively, that friction will present itself at this stage.

✓ *Performing:* The group achieves the goal of generating a solution and presenting it. In groups operating in the professional work environment, this is the most important phase because it is the culmination of the group's efforts. In the group dynamic evaluation, the solution is essentially irrelevant. The important thing to the evaluators is how the group worked together in reaching the solution, and what role each individual member played.

Now that you have a brief overview of how a group typically forms and functions, the question is what role should you play? Should you be the strong leader? The meek wallflower? Somewhere in the middle?

Unfortunately, there's not always a clear-cut answer to that. A lot of it depends on what's happening with your group. In general terms, you must be a <u>contributing</u> member of the group, and you must be friendly and polite while doing it. You need a good combination of communication, timing, and tact. Remember the names of the people in your group and use them. Listen when others speak and look interested.

Be an active member of the group, while maintaining a high level of courtesy at all times. Be very careful about interrupting members of the group when they are speaking, and by "be careful" I mean don't do it.

Courtesy is easy, right? You're a polite person, why is this even worth mentioning? Let's give it a dry run and I'll show you how I've seen applicants have an issue with this. Try to mentally put yourself in the group dynamic setting, and your problem is to nominate a role model. You've though about this a lot (because that question is listed at the end of this section) and you really, really want to nominate Ronald McDonald (picked at random, he's not really my role model). You like Ronald McDonald not just because of his snappy yellow jumpsuit, but because you think grown men that dress like clowns to promote questionably healthy food to children are great role models. Your group is going around the circle voicing their opinions, and it seems like it's taking an eternity to get to you (there are over twenty people in your group, after all). Now the girl across from you in the group is going on and on about Lady Gaga. You notice one of the HR observers is standing right next to you making notes, only you haven't said anything yet. You can feel the tension starting to rise and butterflies start flapping around in the pit of your stomach.

How to Pass the Emirates Cabin Crew Interview

You're worried that you won't be able to get your well-thought-out opinion about Ronald out there, and it seems like your group is running out of time. Now the butterflies have been replaced by a hot and prickly feeling all over your body because the opportunity for the HR reps to notice you is slipping away. The hot prickly feeling starts giving way to panic, and then, almost without you realizing it, something happens:

While the previously mentioned girl is describing Lady Gaga's merits, you blurt out, "I think Ronald McDonald is a great role model because of everything he does for children!"

You talk right over the girl that was speaking. This would be a fail. You've gotten your opinion out there and contributed to the group, but it didn't come out in a very courteous or polite way. All this, despite the fact that you are fundamentally a courteous person. Don't succumb to the pressure. It may not seem like it right now while you're sitting here reading this, but you will feel the pressure on Open Day. Don't under any circumstances interrupt or override other group members. Be patient, wait for a lull in the discussion, or for your turn as they work around the group. Don't force your opinion on the group at an inappropriate time.

Then there's the obvious question of, "should I just try to lead the group?"

It's an easy way to get noticed, there's no doubt. Being out in front leading the group can be a good or bad thing, and there's not really much in-between. Stepping immediately into a leadership role of the group can easily give the impression of being pushy or bossy, which is not what you want to do. Likewise, if you're pushing your opinion too much and not allowing others to effectively voice theirs, it sends an overbearing impression.

In an interview setting, there's a general sense of tension, as everyone wants to be noticed for the right reasons. This can lead to problems. If you have two people in a group, each wanting to make an impression and lead the group, you have a recipe for confrontation. Confrontation in the group dynamic is something you absolutely want to avoid. I have seen group dynamic members get drawn into heated discussions, each pushing their own agenda, and all they ultimately accomplished was ensuring that neither one of them moved on. You've got a short timeframe to come up with an opinion-based answer to a question. Getting drawn into a confrontation over whether Pepsi is a bigger brand that Coke will not look good, nor will it help you accomplish your goal of getting hired.

How to Pass the Emirates Cabin Crew Interview

There's a flip side to that coin, however. There can be a case where NO ONE steps up to provide any direction to the group, and it just flounders around accomplishing nothing. A situation like this doesn't reflect well on anyone in the group, and everyone runs the risk of being cut. Think of it like being on a sinking ship, with everyone sitting around staring at one another as the deck dips below the waves.

All it takes is one person to say, "Hey, maybe we better get on the lifeboats before we all die!"

Then, suddenly, the group springs to action. Sometimes it requires one person get the ball rolling, and a simple statement can be enough.

If your group is going nowhere, you may have to be that person. Here's the secret to group dynamics that most people don't realize: *being a good group leader doesn't mean forcing the group to accept your opinion.* <u>Being a good group leader means guiding the group to effectively form its own opinions, which may or may not be the same as yours.</u> If you find yourself in this situation, make a few statements to put your group on the right path, and then let other members contribute. Don't force your agenda, and be open to what other members have to contribute.

The polar opposite of the group leader is the wallflower. Wallflowers don't make any meaningful contributions to the dynamic, and end up looking unengaged and dull. You can't fade into the background and not help the group achieve the solution. By contribute, I mean that you must do more than just voting "yea" or "nay" for the solution your group puts forward. At some point, you will have to make an intelligent statement with supporting reasons about your opinion. Be ready for it, and make it more than a one-word statement. Try to engage other members of the group, use their names, smile at them, and maintain eye contact. Incorporate all the presentation aspects we've talked about with the members of your group. Pretend that they are your interviewers, because in a way they are. HR reps are observing every aspect of your interaction with one another, and it's all part of the interview.

If you're not leading the group, you will have a chance to voice your opinion. Be patient, and don't force it. Your turn will come, and when it does, be ready with a good idea and a well-spoken point to win your group members over. Even the most belligerent leader is going to go around the table to solicit opinions at some point. Don't let someone else's actions affect your game plan.

Following is a list of example questions from group dynamic exercises. Your group dynamic question may come from this list, but it also MAY NOT! Use this list to practice forming and presenting your opinion, but also be ready to answer a question that is not listed here.

How to Pass the Emirates Cabin Crew Interview

You may already know what I'm going to say, but here it is, anyway: speak your answers and reasons out loud when you practice. Thinking your answer and saying your answer are two different things.

- ✓ Pick a famous role model.
- ✓ What is the world's most iconic brand?
- ✓ Pick one luxury brand that stands above the rest.
- ✓ Apart from computers, PEDS/cell phones - what device changed the world?
- ✓ Who was the world's greatest leader?
- ✓ What was the greatest scientific invention?
- ✓ If you had to choose one medicine, what would it be?
- ✓ What's more important, sports or the arts?
- ✓ What's the greatest movie ever made?
- ✓ What famous person inspires you the most?

Points to remember

- ✓ Interact with your group members the same way you would with your interviewers: be friendly, use your smile, maintain eye contact, remember and use other's names,
- ✓ Communicate effectively with your group using timing, tact, and well formulated statements.
- ✓ Be an active participant without being too pushy.

Yeas or nays

As you may have gleaned from the topics leading up to this point, the yea or nay actually happens continually during the process.

After the group dynamic, there will be another short break, after which all applicants will be given a white strip of paper indicating "Yes" or "No." All applicants are asked not to have an emotional outburst in front of your peers after learning the result.

I know it seems painfully obvious right now, but I'm just going to mention this because it has happened. Do NOT leap into the air and scream "Yes, I knew it!" That seems like a no-brainer, but you will be surprised at how emotionally invested you are in what is written on that tiny strip of white paper. An outburst seems unlikely now, but it can happen (and has happened, and I'm sure will happen again in the future). Focus on staying in control and not showing a lot of emotion one way or the other. Similarly, if your best friend from grade school also gets a "yea," don't engage in a frolicking celebration with them while you are in a public place.

Enjoy the moment quietly if and when you are successful. Congratulate those you have shared the day with who have progressed, even if you have not. You just never know--that same girl you bonded with may be interviewing you when you go back again in a couple of years. The bottom line: act professionally at all times.

Points to remember

- ✓ Act magnanimous in victory, and gracious in defeat.

English comprehension and aptitude tests

English comprehension

If you've read this far, and understood most of it, your English comprehension is pretty good. Like it or not, English is the universal language of aviation. You need to have a high level of proficiency reading, writing, and speaking English. The HR reps will be monitoring use and comprehension of English continuously during the exercises. English comprehension will be tested academically using the TOEFL--Test of English as a Foreign Language.

TOEFL was originally designed as a means of ensuring English language proficiency of non-native students trying to attend a university in the U.S. In addition to universities, the test has since been adopted by many businesses and government agencies to evaluate how well a person comprehends the English language. It was created in 1962 by a council of representatives, blah-blah-blah...

That's all great, but what does it mean to you? The test was created to screen people for whether or not they could attend a university in English. It was created by academics, for an academic setting, and is divided into four sections. Emirates typically only addresses three in their screening:

1. Reading

Typically involves reading several passages that total around 700 words in length. The passages are academic-based topics similar to what you would read in a textbook. The subject of the passage is irrelevant; you don't have to have any prior knowledge of how the North American Shrew Lives in the Wild (for example). The answers to the questions that follow the passage are all contained in the text provided. After reading the text, you will be asked questions about main ideas, details, vocabulary, inferences, etc. You will be given approximately sixty to 100 minutes to complete this section.

2. Speaking

There are two types of tasks in the speaking section: independent and integrated. For independent tasks, speakers are evaluated on their ability to answer opinion questions on topics they are familiar with. In the integrated tasks, you will read a short passage, listen to an academic conversation on the same topic, then answer a question that requires you to combine the information from the text and the talk. Test takers may take notes and then refer back to those notes before giving their responses. A test over this section takes around twenty minutes.

However, because of the large numbers involved on each Open Day, Emirates incorporates this along the way at all stages: question time, resume handover, group dynamics, one-on-one interview

3. Writing

The writing section also contains independent and integrated tasks. For the independent task, you will write an essay that explains and supports your opinion on an issue. The integrated task will require you to read and then write a summary about the important points from the text and how they relate to the passage. This section will take around fifty minutes.

The bottom line to all this is that you have to be proficient in reading, writing, understanding, and speaking English. This book is probably not the easiest one for a non-native English speaker to read, but there's a reason for that. If you run across passages or concepts in here that you don't understand, *don't simply skip over them.* This book is written in a conversational tone for just that reason. Look up words or phrases that you don't understand. You need to be able to grasp the meaning behind what is being written, just as you'll need to communicate with the other members of your groups in English. If you can't keep up with what's being said, it's impossible to be a contributing member to the group.

Watch English language television, listen to English talk-radio, and read some English newspapers online. Most importantly, if English is not the primary language in your area, use it as much as possible. Watching TV in English is not the same as speaking it. I know trying to communicate in a second language is not as much fun as simply listening to the new Rihanna song, or keeping up with Prince William and the royal family, but you've got to be up to speed on your English, there's no simpler way to say it.

How to Pass the Emirates Cabin Crew Interview

Points to remember

✓ Your English proficiency will be evaluated in multiple ways during the screening process. If you feel like there are areas that you need to work on, spend the time leading up to Open Day immersing yourself in as much English language media as possible. And practice! (I know you're sick of hearing me say that by now)

Aptitude and personality tests

Think of a general aptitude test (GAT) as a high school level evaluation of your math and reading skills. It's not exactly an entrance exam for Oxford, but if you haven't done any mathematical story problems in a long time, it can be challenging. You'll be amazed at how quickly you forget algebra when you haven't done it for a few years. That being said, you don't have to be a rocket scientist. The company just wants to make sure that you can formulate thoughts and accomplish tasks without too much difficulty. They want to know that you can work the Duty Free cart to 350 passengers and have the correct amount of receipts and money when you are finished.

There are literally a million GAT study guides and practice quizzes available online. The best way to get up to speed for one of these is...wait for it...*practice beforehand.*

I could write an entirely separate book on studying for these tests because there's such a wide range of topics to cover. You will find many, many study guides and practice tests online that will do a much better job of helping you practice and prepare.

After the knowledge and application tests, there will be a personality inventory test. Here's the important thing to remember about taking personality tests: be yourself and answer honestly. One sure way to screw up a personality assessment is by trying to give the answers you think they want. These tests are specifically designed to weed out those types of answers and the people giving them.

The big picture on how a personality test works is this: a company wants an indicator of how an individual will behave in situations and interact with those around them. Believe it or not, personality tests have actually been shown to be a pretty effective indicator, and companies place a lot of weight on them.

The company will typically look for an applicant that falls within a certain range of scores. For example, anyone who scores between 85-100 (these numbers are arbitrary). The numbers of the score itself aren't important, what matters to you is that there is a MIMIMUM and there can also be a MAXIMUM allowable score to pass. Someone that scores 80 is outside the range, the same as someone that scores 110. What does that mean? Again, don't try to beat the test, and more importantly, follow directions. Most people typically answer personality inventory questions somewhere in the middle of the road, which can ultimately hurt your score. If your answers are too wishy-washy, then you won't make it to the minimum score.

Here's an example of what I'm talking about based on a question the company may consider a *negative trait* in applicants for this position:

> Select a number between 1 and 5, with 1 being "very much like me" and 5 being "not at all like me" in response to the following statement: *I like to sit alone by myself in a room for long periods of time.*

What do you think an appropriate response would be to that question? Think of the question in a big-picture perspective: would this be a desirable quality in someone that has to present a warm, vibrant image to the general public? Probably not. Someone that answers 1 (very much like me) would have points detracted from their total score, while someone that answers 5 (very much like me) would have points added toward the total.

Some applicants will over-think this question, "Well, I don't really like to sit alone in my room, but there are times when I do it. Like when I'm sleeping. Maybe this question is trying to find out if I'm lying or not? I'll just put a 3."

An answer of 3, in this particular example, is exactly in the middle of the scale. When the test is scored, a middle scale answer won't hurt you by detracting any points, but it won't help you by adding any either. If all your answers are in the middle of the scale, especially to personality traits you obviously should have, you won't meet the minimum score. Have some conviction in your answers--don't take the middle of the road for every response.

After these tests, successful applicants will continue on to the one on one interview.

How to Pass the Emirates Cabin Crew Interview

Points to remember

- ✓ Unless you're currently teaching a high school math and English class, do some online preparation for your GAT.
- ✓ Don't try to beat a personality test by giving the answers you think that they want. At the same time, if you feel strongly about a statement or question, then make sure it comes across in your answers. If you fail to answer with enough conviction, it can hurt your score.

Advanced group dynamic

The total number of applicants has thinned out by this point. The group size for the second dynamic is typically around five to eight members. Each member of the group will be given a paper and pencil to make notes about the scenario. The HR reps will read the scenario only ONCE, so pay attention and take down as many details as possible. The time for this group exercise is set at about twenty minutes, which adds to the pressure.

What's happening in this group dynamic, and what's different from the first one? The scenario is designed to create some conflict among group members, as it can typically be a life and death situation (examples follow this section). There is a need to comprehend the situation dictated in English, follow directions, take notes, and adhere to a strict timeline. Last, but not least, is the ever-present observation and evaluation on how you interact with the respective member of your group.

As with the previous exercise, be on your best behavior at all times. Don't interrupt other group members, even if you don't agree with what their saying. Let members voice their positions, then voice yours. Use good body language, smile, and maintain eye contact with all members in the group when you speak.

With this scenario, again, there is no right or wrong answer. The HR reps are more focused on whether you comprehend the situation, how the dynamics of your group develop, how you work together through the problem, and how you reach the resolution.

This exercise is more structured and requires more cooperation among the members. In exercises like this, there are several different roles that members fall into within the group:

- ✓ Group leader
- ✓ Note taker
- ✓ Time keeper
- ✓ Member

By group member, I'm referring to a member of the group that doesn't perform any of the other specific functions listed. Members contribute to the group, add their viewpoints, but don't necessarily drive the direction of the group or take the notes. There is nothing wrong with being a good contributing member, so don't feel like you have to forge ahead and be the leader, especially if you're not comfortable or used to that role.

As far as being the leader, we've discussed the positive and negative aspects of that previously, and the same rules apply here.

Note taker (or record keeper) will be a required position here. You may have to come up with a list of items An example is things you want to have on a deserted island. Someone will have to step forward to take these notes. This is a good position to be in: it shows some initiative in taking on the workload, and allows you to sit back and listen to all the group members while still contributing in the form of taking accurate notes. Operative word there being "accurate." Don't say that you want to be the note taker and then take all the wrong notes. That doesn't look good.

Time Keeper is another valuable position. You've got twenty minutes to work through this problem. That may sound like a lot when you're sitting here reading this, but it goes by quickly, I assure you. If you don't have a member of your group specifically assigned to watch the clock, I can almost guarantee you'll reach the time limit and not have the entire solution. Someone needs to keep the group on track and within the limit. Like being the note taker, this is a good position to volunteer for. It's important and easy at the same time. Just don't forget to *actually* watch the clock.

Some people in the group may assume more than one role.

Sometimes the person taking the notes also ends up being the leader, and that's fine provided that you're not trying to "do everything yourself." If there is a void for one of the positions and no one steps in to fill it, you'd better, because a floundering group is just as bad as a confrontational one.

Here's a personal example: I was being observed in a group dynamic, exactly like the one you're going to be doing. I had a clear game plan in my head of how I wanted to handle it, and it was all the advice I've just given you. The one thing I did not want to do was forge ahead and be the leader, because I felt like that was too high visibility, and I didn't want the liability that came along with it (if the members of your group are totally dysfunctional, you're the leader of a dysfunctional group, and that's that).

Our problem was to pick an astronaut for a mission from a list of candidates (not a problem you will get, but similar in nature). We were given a long list of all the requirements the candidate, and told that only one candidate out of eight met all those requirements. Our job was to figure out which applicant was the correct choice. They handed out papers, each paper had the profile of an astronaut applicant and some (but not all) of the requirements for the mission. The point of the exercise was to see if a group of strangers could work effectively as a group, pool all the information we had together, and come up with the correct solution. All in twenty minutes. After the HR reps handed out the papers, everyone started quietly reading theirs, without saying a word. I finished reading mine and put it down on the table, folding my hands on the paper, and waited for the others.

I decided long before going into this exercise that I wasn't going to jump out in front of the firing squad and be the first person to say something. I didn't want to come of as that pushy guy that needs to be in charge. So I sat there quietly waiting, and I watched as each member of the group finished reading and set their paper down on the table, just like me, and then said nothing.

I was literally screaming inside my head, "COME ON! SOMEONE DO SOMETHING!"

The clock was ticking...we were almost five minutes into the exercise by now...and no one in the group had said one word to anyone else.

As much as I didn't want to be the one to start, our group was going nowhere, and that wasn't a good situation.

So I jumped on the hand grenade and said, "How about we go around the table and everyone can list what they have for the astronaut requirements?"

That was all it took, just like the sinking ship example I gave you a little while ago. One sentence and everyone jumped on board. A guy facing the clock volunteered to watch the time, and he gave us notifications every five minutes. The person at the head of the table started reading from their sheet. I said I would keep the notes, again because no one was volunteering to do so. We worked through the problem and came up with a solution right at the twenty minute mark.

I still to this day don't know if we picked the right candidate. They told us there was only one right answer, and my gut feeling at the time was that we hadn't picked the right one. As we've discussed with group dynamics in interview settings, the answer itself isn't as important as the method that you use to arrive at it. Incidentally, the only two people that advanced from that group were myself and the timekeeper.

After this group exercise, applicants continuing on to the next phase will be notified. You're close, but not quite done by this stage. Make sure previous rules for notification apply.

Here are some example scenarios from the advanced group dynamic. You might not get something exactly as listed, but it will almost undoubtedly be similar:

- ✓ You all wash up on a small lush tropical deserted island in the middle of the Pacific Ocean. You will not be saved for one month. Choose one item to have with you from the following three: canopy, fishing rod, or water purification kit. Discuss and deliver the answer in twenty minutes.

- ✓ You were staying at a remote cabin in northern Finland during the winter (why would you do that?), but unfortunately for you, it has burned down. The airplane that picks you up is not due back for two weeks, and a major storm is moving into your area. You must make a physically demanding five-day trek to safety. You have full winter gear and tents, ample water with the snow and streams, and a small gas flamed cooking stove. You are the leaders of the group. You can only choose one of two food packs to take: low fat granola bars or vacuum packed meat. Half of your group does not eat meat for religious reasons. Food pack choices are only just enough for the five day duration of your trip. Pick one.

- ✓ Your group is in a life raft after your yacht has sunk. You are in the middle of the Indian Ocean. There are twenty-two items in the raft, and you can only pick 15 to help you survive (There are various items, all relevant to survival).

- ✓ You are starting a colony on a new planet. There are ten other colonies on the same planet. An assembly has been arranged where each colony will be represented by a leader. Your leader must be smart, strong, articulate, and will need to work well with the other leaders to achieve your colony's objective. Elect a leader.

Points to remember

- ✓ You must participate in the group exercise. You don't HAVE to be the leader, timekeeper, or note-taker, but you must make a meaningful contribution.
- ✓ All the rules from previous exercises apply: while making your contributions, you must be polite, friendly, and well spoken.

One on one interview

Welcome to the final hurdle in your quest to become a cabin crew member with Emirates. This particular event causes a lot of anxiety, but it shouldn't. You should be excited about this interview. You don't have to navigate the intricacies of group interaction or do problem solving anymore. You don't have to sit down in front of a computer and try to remember the Pythagorean theorem. All you have to do now is have a conversation about how much you'd like to be a cabin crew member.

If you've made it to this point, then you are meeting and interacting with people effectively. This event shouldn't be any different. All the previous rules of presentation and common courtesy continue to apply. Don't change what you're doing (it's obviously working), but don't make the assumption that the job is in the bag, either. All the time and effort you've invested in the process has served to get you to this singular event, the chance to sit down personally with an HR representative and show them that you are the person they want. If you need a target for your interview performance to peak at, it's during this one-on-one interview.

This is where it should all come together: good solid handshake, confident demeanor, consistent eye contact, and courteous and well-spoken interactions.

Presentation aspects aside, let's talk about how to prepare for this interview and the questions that you'll be asked. There are typically some core questions interviewers will ask, but the reality is that they can ask anything that pops into their head. The questions can range from, "Why do you want to live in Dubai?" to "If you were an animal, what would you be?" The important thing about answering these questions is to know beforehand that *there is no way to prepare an answer for each and every question they may ask.*

Wait, if I can't prepare and answer, what good is this stupid book I'm reading?

Here's the good news: you don't have to prepare for each and every answer, you just need to have a framework in place for how to answer questions. The elements for having an effective framework in place is everything we've talked about up to now. If you have been practicing, and by practicing I mean physically verbalizing answers to questions, your framework of skills will be ready. Consider this phase of this interview just like sitting down and having a conversation with someone at a coffee shop.

Your demeanor should be one of relaxed professionalism. I know you want this job very much. *They* know you want this job very much. You want to avoid acting desperate, however. Act like you would love to have the job (which you do, of course), but you have to also act like not getting the job isn't the end of the world.

There are two core styles an interviewer can adopt (every other interview tactic is a variation of these two themes): friendly interview or confrontational interview. You need to be ready for either or both of them.

Friendly interviewers are very warm, calm, and casual, which seems nice. This is the type of interview most people prefer, if given the choice. Don't allow an interviewer's casual demeanor to disarm you and draw you in to acting casual, as well. If an interviewer talks or acts with informality that doesn't mean you can. This method is designed to do exactly that, see if they can make you relax and draw you in to behaving unprofessionally. Don't allow them to change the way you perform in your interview. Interview professionalism rules *always* apply, all the way until you leave the building.

Then you have the confrontational interview. A confrontational interview is not meant to make you feel comfortable, just the opposite. They are trying to rattle you and see if they can throw you off your game. The interviewer's demeanor will not be friendly, just coolly professional.

How to Pass the Emirates Cabin Crew Interview

Their questions will be similar to, "Why should we hire you?" and "What do you have the someone else doesn't?" Don't worry if your interviewer doesn't act friendly, but don't under any circumstances allow that to cause you to not act friendly. Remember the job you're applying for: not every person you deal with is going to be pleasant, but you have to present the same happy, vibrant face to everyone. That is the point of the confrontational interview: Can you keep your composure under pressure? Make sure you do, and make sure you are smiling even if your interviewer is not.

You want to be friendly, outgoing, and conversational, while still limiting your answers to an appropriate length. Focus on formulating your answers to these questions as if you were writing a short essay. Give the thesis statement, which is essentially re-stating the question you've been asked, then give two or three supporting statements, at the most. Keep your statements direct and to the point.

You'll want to have done some research for the one-on-one interview. They're going to ask you why you want to work for this particular airline. You should have some knowledge of its history, and where it's going in the future. You can find all this information on the company's Web site, and you should have a thorough knowledge of the company itself prior to the interview. Read about its history, and look through recent press releases. Companies generally publish press releases about events they're proud of, and if you read something significant, make a note of it. If the company just ordered 100 new jets, that is a good reason to want to join. If they just posted record-breaking profits, again, another good reason to join.

You're applying for a job that will require you to live as an expatriate, most likely in Dubai. There will be some questions on how you feel about that. You should have a working knowledge of the region, the United Arab Emirates, and Dubai in particular. There are many social and economic advantages to living and working in the UAE, so have a list in your head of what those advantages are because they will come up.

Sometimes individuals can have a hard time living and working overseas, particularly if you're from a tight (close) family. A popular line of questioning is how you will cope with living away from your family, so you'll want to have convincing reasons for why this won't be an issue for you.

If you do a little research into the subject areas above, the rest is just having a spontaneous conversation. The most important aspect with these answers is not to script a response. When someone has a scripted response to a particular question, it is obvious. You can (and

How to Pass the Emirates Cabin Crew Interview

should) have some ideas about the direction you want to go with a particular answers, but it should be more of a rough outline than a script.

Here is a list of questions you can use to prepare. Again, don't have a scripted answer to any of these; your answer should be slightly different each time (as it would in a normal conversation). Use this list to get an idea of the important elements that you want to touch on in your answers. Have a rough outline in your head of points you want to cover.

1. Why do you want to work for XXX Airlines?
2. Why do you want to be a cabin crew member?
3. How do you feel about living overseas?
4. How will you deal with living away from your family?
5. Who is your role model?
6. Will you enjoy living in Dubai?
7. What do you know about Dubai?
8. What is a burka?
9. What does your family think about this?
10. What do you think the most difficult part the job is?
11. Have you ever shared an apartment with a stranger?
12. Have you ever worked shift hours?
13. What is your strongest/weakest point?
14. What is Ramadan?

15. Do you know the difference between an Airbus and a Boeing?

16. Do you have any friends at Emirates?

17. Where have you travelled in your life?

18. Tell me about your educational background.

19. Where do you see yourself in three, five, ten years time?

20. Do you have any family members currently employed in aviation?

Points to remember

- ✓ If you've made it this far, don't change what you've been doing.
- ✓ You're interviewer may be friendly, or they may not. Maintain your professional presentation regardless of the feedback you're getting.
- ✓ Review facts about the United Arab Emirates, Dubai, and Emirates prior to your interview. You will use these facts when formulating your answers.
- ✓ Don't try to memorize a scripted answer for interview questions. Have an idea of what you want to say, but don't memorize a script to say it. Your answers should be semi-spontaneous and conversational.

Closing the interview

By this point in the process, you may feel like you've just run a marathon uphill while pushing a boulder. The finish line is in sight; don't jeopardize all your hard work by quitting too early. When your interviewer thanks you, don't just stand up, mumble thanks under your breath, and stumble out of the room. Closing the interview is just as important as everything else.

A standard interview courtesy is for the person evaluating you to ask if you have any questions at the end of the process. Having a (Good!) question in mind is a good idea, as it can show insight and involvement on your part. Good questions are typically ones involving the company, recent press releases, hiring projections, that kind of thing. Some very general examples:

- ✓ I noticed the company placed a large order for new aircraft, is that to accommodate expansion or to replace older aircraft?
- ✓ How many cabin crewmembers do you anticipate hiring this year?
- ✓ Typically how long would it take to reach the position of purser?
- ✓ Are there opportunities to branch out into other departments within Emirates?

- ✓ Are there specific sport activity clubs active in Dubai, i.e., sailing, cycling, windsurfing, etc?
- ✓ Are there any plans for Emirates to expand/start service to this country?

Bad questions are controversial subjects, anything that has been covered in detail previously in a prior presentation, personal interests, or anything that gives the impression that you don't understand your role in the big picture of the organization. Don't ask if there's political unrest in the Middle East, if Dubai is dangerous, or if Emirates anticipates being in business two years from now.

Aside from asking a question if offered, there is an old tried and true sales technique that says at the end of your presentation, ask for the business. This whole interview process has been your presentation, so take a moment at the close to tell your interviewer how much you would enjoy working for their company. Again, don't come across as desperate or begging for the job, but a simple statement saying the company is something you would enjoy being part of is sufficient. Close your interview with a firm handshake, good eye contact, and a solid and sincere thank-you.

How to Pass the Emirates Cabin Crew Interview

Now comes the hard part: waiting for your results. Most applicants are told to wait a minimum of fourteen days. Some wait up to six weeks to learn their results. Waiting is no fun, but there's no way around it. Making it though the entire interview process is an accomplishment in and of itself.

Physicals

I've mentioned a couple of times that there will be two physical examinations: one in your home country and one in Dubai. You're not going to be able to hide anything in the final and more thorough examination. What that means is: don't lie about something that would disqualify you, because they will find out about it. Just because you've come all the way to UAE, don't think they're going to overlook the snake tattoo on your neck that you covered up with makeup in the assessment. They won't, and you'll be on a plane back home. Honesty is the best policy.

How to Pass the Emirates Cabin Crew Interview

One aspect of the physical is a drug screen, so consider this: when you are leaving your home to go live and work in Dubai, all your friends are going to want to go out and have one last good time before you leave. Just don't have TOO good a time. You will be drug screened during your initial physical and AGAIN when you arrive in Dubai. It is a mandatory requirement from the Civil Aviation Authorities of the UAE that all new crew members be tested again when they initiate residency. Don't throw away your opportunity by doing something stupid before you leave to start your new career. You will be drug screened during your medical when you arrive in Dubai, keep that in mind when saying your goodbyes.

Conclusion

We've reached the end. I know we've covered a lot of ground, and your head may be swimming a bit with all that it takes to be successful in a cabin crew interview. That's OK. Give yourself some time to process all the information here, then revisit this book as your Open Day draws near.

The most important fact you can remember is this: there is no one aspect, no silver bullet, and no trick you can use to fool your interviewers into hiring you. To be a successful applicant, you must represent the "total package." Try not to focus on *one area* we've covered here, and instead focus on combining *everything* together. If your resume is perfect but your suit looks terrible, you won't get the job. The opposite is also true: a great looking suit and terrible paperwork aren't a good combination. Emirates is looking for the perfect combination of all the aspects we've covered in their cabin crew, and they have a huge applicant pool to draw from.

Take the time and effort to show up as prepared as you can. That's the best anyone can do. If you've given 100% of the effort you can to get this job, then you'll sleep well at night know you've done everything you can. Good luck in your efforts.

If this is really what you want to do, never give up chasing the dream.

Believe me, it's worth it. See you on board.

Printed in France by Amazon
Brétigny-sur-Orge, FR